REACHING
YOUR
POTENTIAL

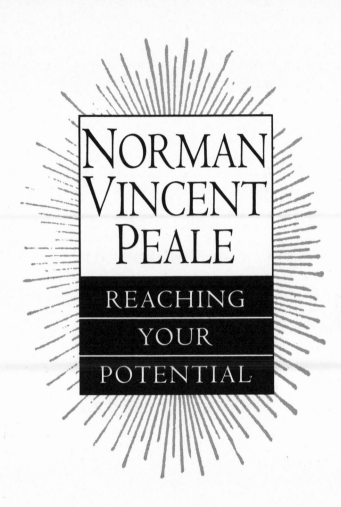

NORMAN VINCENT PEALE

REACHING

YOUR

POTENTIAL

WINGS BOOKS
New York • Avenel, New Jersey

This 1997 edition is published by Wings Books,
a division of Random House Value Publishing, Inc.,
40 Engelhard Avenue, Avenel, New Jersey 07001,
by arrangement with Baker Book House, Inc.

Wings Books and colophon are trademarks of
Random House Value Publishing, Inc.

Random House
New York • Toronto • London • Sydney • Auckland
http://www.randomhouse.com/

Printed and bound in the United States of America

Library of Congress Cataloging-in-Publication Data

Peale, Norman Vincent, 1898-1993.
    [How to be your best]
    Reaching your potential / Norman Vincent Peale.
        p.   cm.
    Previously published: Tarrytown, N.Y. : F.H. Revell, c1990
    ISBN 0-517-18542-3
        1. Reformed Church in America—Sermons. 2. Sermons, American.
    3. Reformed Church—Sermons. 4. Self—actualization (Psychology)-
    -Religious aspects—Christianity—Sermons.   I. Title.
    [BX9527.P43H5   1997]
    252' .05732—dc20   96-31514
                                                                    CIP

8   7   6   5   4   3   2   1

CONTENTS

FOREWORD

These days there seems to be a lot of confusion about whether there are any permanent truths to hang on to. So much is changing, and in the course of my life I have certainly witnessed many profound changes in this world.

But I have discovered that some things do not change. Because of that, I can write this book based on enduring principles that I have built upon in my lifetime.

First, I have found that the spiritual help available through Jesus Christ is the same today as fifty years ago. If anything, the method of living I have called "Positive Thinking" has gained greater acceptance throughout the years.

Second, the simple formulas for applying this spiritual guidance to everyday life are the same today as when I started to preach the Gospel. As we worked on this book, I asked myself, would people in the 1990s, trying the same methods, achieve the same results as someone I told about in 1970? It was exciting to answer that question with a resounding *yes*, because everywhere I travel today I hear similar stories of powerful results in the lives of people from many walks of life.

Third, the hurts and needs of people stay the same. Our clothes may change, or the ways we earn a living, or our method of travel. (I used to go everywhere by train and thereby met many interesting people.) But the basic human problems of inferiority, loneliness, worry, fear, tension, and doubt never change. I suppose they have not changed much since the beginning of time.

So, you are holding the result of those three discoveries. These concepts work when you work them; they are timeless; people still have the same needs that provoked the development of these ideas. My positive prayer for you is that you will find something for your life.

If I could get across just one concept, it would be this: *You are someone special because you have divine potential within you just waiting to blossom.*

Once you start with that idea, nothing can hold you back, because you will start to see yourself as God does: a person of wonder and beauty. You will find the source of positive attitudes that lead to belief, faith, hope, anticipation, enthusiasm—in a word, LIFE.

By now, I'm sure you have deduced that the germination of the material for this book came to me as I performed my function as a minister of the Christian Gospel. These days, there seems to be uncertainty about what preachers should preach and whether the teachings of Jesus are valid today.

To me, Jesus is simply the greatest personality who ever lived. He has the greatest thoughts of any philosopher. He has the greatest wisdom of any counselor. He has the deepest insight of any psychiatrist. But most of all, He has the greatest love possible for every man, woman, or child who was ever born.

Perhaps He summed it up best when He described His purpose in coming to this earth and walking among men. He knew that many negative forces would press upon mankind. He called these forces "thieves" who set upon unsuspecting lambs:

"The thief does not come except to steal, and to kill, and to destroy: *I am come that they may have life and that they may have it more abundantly*" (*see* John 10:10).

Abundant life! What a wonderful concept. That life is open to you.

Norman Vincent Peale

Norman Vincent Peale
Pawling, NY

REACHING
YOUR
POTENTIAL

ONE

A POSITIVE ATTITUDE WORKS WONDERS

Any person who needs a change within himself, or within his life, can have this take place by changing his mind. This, however, cannot be superficial mental change; it must be in-depth. Such a change can be extremely effective.

Are you, perhaps, facing a hard situation? Are you involved in some unsatisfactory personal relationship? Is there some other kind of trouble in your life? We could hardly enumerate all the problems a human being has to deal with. But there is a great answer to them all, and it is this: They can all be changed and you can be changed—everything for the better—through the magic of a positive mental attitude.

Now, a positive mental attitude, a phrase coined by my dear friend W. Clement Stone, is not just some cheery, blithe point of view. A truly positive attitude faces all the cold, hard realities of a situation and sees them straight. It does not desire to evade them—because it knows it can handle them. A positive mental attitude is positive think-ing in-depth. It is vertical thinking: it rises to God, comes back to you, back to God, back to you; the power passes along a vertical line and, lest you think this is some kind of psychological dissertation, there is a text from the Bible that supports it. Romans 12:2 says, "Be ye transformed by the renewing of your mind." That means if you don't like the way you are now, you can change yourself by making a fundamental change in your mind.

Let us imagine a difficult situation. There does not seem to be any hope in it, any possibility, any potential. Now, let's bring two men with different points of view up against it. One has a negative attitude and the other a positive attitude. The man with the negative attitude will immediately, of course, be appalled by it. He will see no chance of light in the darkness. It is all impossible. It's hopeless. There is no chance of doing anything with it. So naturally, a series of unhappy circumstances develops from it. What else could he expect? His negative outlook em-phasizes every destructive aspect of the situation. He is an expert at that.

Now, on the other hand, a man with a positive attitude, facing precisely the same situation, asks himself some ques-tions. He is no Pollyanna. He knows the score; he sees the difficulties. But he asks himself, *What is God trying to say to me through this tough situation? There is an answer here, and I mean to find it. I know that, with the help of God, I can handle this situation and turn it to happy results.* Consequently, from the situation flow bright and happy potentials.

Isn't it strange—or is it? What makes the difference? It is how you think about something. It is whether you bring to a situation (personal, business, social, or whatever it may be) the magic of a positive mental attitude.

I admire the industrialist Henry Kaiser. He was a great big man, physically, spiritually, and mentally. He came from humble beginnings, but he had been raised in a Christian home, with a positive Christian spirit, and he believed that with the help of God you could accomplish anything. He had a principle that anything you can conceive, you can achieve. It was said of him that he never knew when something couldn't be done, which is a remarkable virtue to have.

During World War II, this country had to have more ships and have them fast, and the shipbuilding companies couldn't produce enough. Their methods were too slow. Kaiser came forward and offered to build them. Now, he had never built a ship, but ships were needed, and he was an American, and he believed that God would help him do it. I was at the meeting where he told a whole ballroom full of leading industrialists how he was going to build what they called "liberty ships." Some men sitting near me made the most uncomplimentary remarks about Mr. Kaiser: "He's a fool. He knows nothing about ships. How can he build them?" But Kaiser did build them, because he didn't know he couldn't!

There are so many people around today saying that society is going to pieces and the country is going down the drain. Let us hope these people never become the majority in this country—or we will be through. Fortunately, we still have people who believe that, out of all the tumult of this hour, we will build a greater world than ever before. With a positive attitude, the minds of all people can be transformed so they will see things from the standpoint of new and more profound justice and brotherhood than ever before. And these things will come to pass. A positive mental attitude—it's a magical thing!

I was reading the sports pages of the newspaper one day. These I enjoy even more than the front pages, because you know that there are pretty decent people on the sports pages. If you read the sports pages, you can stand the front pages. Anyway, I was reading about a football player named Tom Dempsey, who was then playing for the New Orleans Saints. He had just single-handedly won a game over the New York Giants. He was twenty-two years old and considered by some the greatest field-goal kicker in the game. With un-erring accuracy, he would boot the ball right over the cross-bar. He was a genius with the foot—because he was also a genius with the mind.

His foot was motivated by a positive attitude, for Tom Dempsey, big fine husky chap that he is, was born with a right hand without fingers and a half-formed right foot. He had to wear an orthopedic kicking shoe that cost him two hundred dollars. But with that half foot, he made incredible kicks. One sportswriter asked him, "How do you do so well, being handicapped?"

"What's that you say?" he asked. "I don't know the

word. I never thought of myself as being handicapped. And, as for the word *can't,* it's not in my vocabulary."

Now, how about you? Your difficulty, little or big—is it bigger than you? Or are you bigger than it? "Be ye transformed by the renewing of your mind." Know that, with Jesus Christ, all things are possible, *all* things; and you will be the beneficiary of the magic of a positive mental attitude.

What is it that undergirds this positive attitude? It is nothing dreamy or Pollyannaish; it is a solid fact, a fact that should be brought again and again to the attention of us all. It is the fact of who you are. Who are you? You are a child of God. You are a being in time and eternity.

You have a physical body and this physical body is a marvelous instrument. We take it too much for granted. Only God could have thought of the physical body. Only God could have created it. Look what it can do. Take, for example, a hand. It may seem ordinary. But look at the various positions and motions you can make with your fingers and your hand. You can turn it down and you can raise it up; you can reach behind and sideways. Think of the angles, the joints, the engineering that goes into that one small member of your body known as a hand! And that isn't all there is about you. There is the heart and the central nervous system. There is the blood vessel system and the bone structure. And this wonderful body isn't the greatest thing about you, either.

There is in you that indescribable thing called God's

power. It is a power over yourself, a power over situations, a power over circumstances. If you exercise this power, amazing things can be done. It is through the use of a positive mental attitude that you have such power. Now, you must be humble about it. It isn't *your* power. It is God living within you. This is why we constantly urge people to come into a closer relationship with Jesus Christ. Why? He releases power, whereby anyone can manage himself and make a contribution through this inner thing called spiritual power.

One of the first stories ever published in *Guideposts* magazine was by aviator Eddie Rickenbacker, who was a great American and a sincere Christian. He titled the article "I Believe in Prayer," and he told how, in his adventurous life, the power of prayer had enabled him to face death a dozen times, look it right in the eye, and live. He said this was one of the things that made him believe in a protective Providence and in life after death.

He related an experience he had while driving a racing car, many years ago, on a speedway. He had it going at the top of its power. He was leading the pack, driving skillfully. Suddenly he felt a faint tremor in the mechanism. Now, he knew that, if anything went wrong at that speed, it could mean disaster and possibly death. But instead of thinking disaster, he prayed in confidence and faith. He sent up the vertical thought to God. And suddenly, he said, he had one of the greatest experiences of his life. He knew exultantly that he had power over that machine, that he could bring it in even if it deteriorated—he could bring it in, driving it not by his hands but by his mind. Rickenbacker said that if he had told other drivers of this, they would have thought he was crazy. He knew that there is built into a human being an enormous power, if he will but use it.

I once went with Rickenbacker to a hospital to speak to airmen who had been sent back from the fighting front, many of them broken in body and in spirit. I'll never forget him standing there, as he spoke to those airmen about the power God had put in them. He told them they mustn't give in to depression or defeat in the face of any problem. He closed his speech in this manner: "Let me tell you guys something," he said. (They all had their eyes riveted on him.) "If you haven't had an experience of God in your life, you get yourself one mighty quick, because with that you will have power over all your problems."

"Well," you say, "Rickenbacker was an extraordinary person." That is right. But so are you, if you will allow yourself to be. The trouble is that many people write themselves off as ordinary. But God never made an ordinary human being. Maybe you think you never could have power like this. But you really can, if you believe you can.

I once made a speech to a chamber of commerce in a southern city, and it was recorded for a radio broadcast later on. When I went back to my hotel to get my bag, I heard a radio playing in the lobby, and I recognized my own voice. I saw there weren't many people in the lobby, so I sat down behind a pillar to listen to my own speech, just to see how it sounded. After listening for a little while, I decided to go upstairs to my room and get my bag.

Now, the girl running the elevator was leaning there, chewing gum. I got in the elevator, and presently she pulled herself together and got in to run it up for me. I asked her, "Did you listen to that speech on the radio there in the lobby?"

"Yeah," she answered, "I listened to it."

"What did you think of it?"

"Well," she replied, "that man sure does like to hear himself talk, doesn't he?"

"You don't know me, do you?" I asked. And she said no, she didn't, for which I was profoundly grateful!

God never made an ordinary human being.

Well, I got my bag and, on the way down, I talked with this elevator operator again. She said, "You know that speech by that man?"

"The one who likes to hear himself talk?"

"Yes, sir, that's the one." She continued, "You know, there was one little point that got to me. It was pretty good."

"What was that?" I asked.

"Well," she said, "you know what he said? He said,

'Everyone has something greater in him than he ever knew.' "

"You think you've got that in you?"

"Yes, sir. I know I have, and someday I'm going to go places."

Well, that was the last I ever saw of her. But from the look in her eyes and that sense of latent power she expressed, I have no doubt that the positive mental attitude, if cultivated, can give her power over her problems.

God has planted this potential in you and me, and it will never rest until it is realized—until you get yourself "transformed by the renewing of your mind" through Christ. It is Christ who does it. The greatest thing that can happen to anyone is to accept Christ, to find Him, to have Him explode in your mind, to become identified with Him. He is not merely the head of a religious faith or someone whose picture is in stained-glass windows. He is a vital principle. And when this principle connects with a human being, a great transformation takes place. There is romance in the way people's lives can be changed through Christ. A man is weak, defeated, sinful, confused, and everything suffers accordingly. All of a sudden, God comes into this man's mind and soul and works a transformation, a miracle, and the man is changed. He is no longer the same person. Everyone can become a changed person by the power of God and the magic of a positive mental attitude.

Some years ago, I was speaking in a church in New Jersey on a Sunday afternoon. Sitting in the pulpit before speaking, looking at the congregation, I noticed the face of a certain man. The minute my eye caught his eye, he smiled at me and I smiled at him. And I sat there thinking about him, for this man is a miracle of transformation. There was a time when he was really licked and had become a heavy drinker, for that was the only way he felt he could live with himself. Everything was at loose ends. He was mixed up, hopeless, and running low on money. It was one job after another and all that disorganized kind of living.

Well, one day he was slumped over a bar in Brooklyn, as he describes it, about half shot. There was a radio in the bar and it was tuned—get this—to one of my sermons. And he was listening. Now, thousands of people listen to sermons and nothing happens. But once in a while something does. So here he was slumped over a bar. And something was said in that sermon about the immense possibilities of a human being who would accept God into his life to reorganize him.

The next Sunday, this man came to Marble Collegiate Church, and he was there every Sunday thereafter for a long time. He became a member of the young adult group. His life was completely changed. But, he said, it was not in the church or in the group that the change occurred. He was changed in that bar when an idea penetrated his consciousness and exploded in his mind. The explosion was from the sudden belief that God could change him. He experienced then and there the magic of a positive mental attitude.

Now, however the change takes place, it is valid. If you live your days thinking on an elevated, positive level with

God, everything, including yourself, will change. Problems that you couldn't handle before, you now will be able to handle. Situations that previously you couldn't endure, you now will be able to endure or even change. Accept this concept. Tell yourself, "I will live with the magic of a positive mental attitude through the help of the Lord Jesus Christ." You'll never be the same person again—you will be a new person.

TWO
BE YOURSELF!

If you travel the whole world over, in country after country, amid the teeming millions of this earth, you will never find a person quite like yourself. And that isn't the whole story. To the best of our knowledge, from the beginning of time, *there has never been anyone quite like you.*

Furthermore, a genetic scientist has said that if you had 300 *billion* brothers and sisters, none of them would be exactly like you. What a marvel and a wonder of creation you are! When you look at yourself in the mirror you can say, "I am unique. There has never been another person quite like me."

Now, if you stop at that, you are likely to build up egotism, which isn't the idea. This uniqueness of the individual lays a tremendous responsibility on you and on me. I should say to myself, "I am different; I have a job to do in this world. If I do not do it, it will never be done." And you, too, have a job to do in this world. If you do not do it, it will never be done. There is no one quite like you. And I repeat, this is the wonder and the marvel of divine creation.

It is a good thing God made man, rather than man making man, for God has a sense of the uniqueness of the individual. If man had made man, we would probably all have been standardized types from a vast assembly line, with no infinite variation, no profound difference. God's creation of man is another example of the vast respect He has for each human being.

God tell us, in 2 Corinthians 5:17, how to realize ourselves: "If any man be in Christ, he is a new creature: old things are passed away; behold, all things are become new."

Now, how do we realize this uniqueness? First, the only way to approximate the greatness implicit in human creation is to *be yourself.* One of the basic laws of human existence is this: *Find yourself, know yourself, be yourself.* If any generation of people needs to relearn this lesson, it is the American people today. Historically, we regard ourselves as the greatest nation of creative individuals in the history of mankind. This nation became great because it stimulated individuals who regarded themselves, under God, as uncrowned kings. But through the years this idea has been

---

If you try to imitate someone else, you become

second-rate. All great thinkers are people

who dare to be themselves.

---

eroded. A social concept has developed that depreciates individualism. Why the two cannot walk together is difficult to understand. But now we have become a generation of imitators; no one must be different from anyone else.

It is a dangerous thing to be an imitator. Ralph Waldo Emerson, in his famous essay on self-reliance, says, "Imitation is suicide." This means, I believe, that if you try to be anyone other than yourself, you kill your own personality; you actually kill your own soul. I sometimes think we ought to bring a bill into Congress changing our national symbol from the eagle to the buffalo, because we are more like the buffaloes today than we are like the eagles. The eagle is a powerful bird. He flies alone. He rises up with authority into the sky. He is master of all he surveys. He is an individualist and was selected in the old days from among the rest of the birds to be our symbol. But the buffalo was never alone. He always ran in a herd with the rest of the buffaloes. And friends, I call to your attention that the buffaloes are gone from the open range, but the eagles are still here.

The lesson is clear: Any nation that becomes a nation of the herd ceases to produce great figures. If ever the idea comes to your mind, *Don't be different, because people will think I am peculiar,* remember what Emerson said: "Imitation is suicide." If you try to imitate someone else, you become second-rate. All great thinkers are people who dare to be themselves.

I read once about the American musician George Gershwin. Gershwin idolized the great Irving Berlin. He was a struggling composer, getting about thirty-five dollars a week in New York City's Tin Pan Alley, and Berlin noticed him. Berlin offered him a job as his musical secretary at three times thirty-five dollars a week. But he said, "George, I advise you not to take this job, because if you do, you will become a second-rate Irving Berlin. But if you say to yourself, 'I, George Gershwin, am unique, and I'll be nobody else but George Gershwin,' you can become immortal." And that was exactly what he did.

Years ago, I watched the life story of Willie Mays on television. He is one of the greatest athletes baseball ever produced. But he wasn't always like that. Willie Mays idolized Joe DiMaggio. He watched how DiMaggio stood, how he walked, how he swung the bat, how he ran; he tried his best to be another DiMaggio. Finally, some wise coach said to him, "Willie, you have great ability. Don't be like anybody else. Be yourself." And he became Willie Mays. If you were to name the greatest players in the history of baseball, no list would be complete without the name of this man who became himself.

Almighty God put a personality in you, different from any other He ever made. And He means for you to bring it out, to let it loose. Be yourself.

My wife and I were once invited to dinner by friends who live in a swanky Park Avenue apartment. It was quite a place, but even in such well-appointed homes things can go wrong. The cook became ill at the last minute and we had to be taken out for dinner. By this time it was about nine o'clock. The restaurant we entered was so dimly lit that you almost needed a flashlight to find your seat. Under the cover of darkness, I asked my wife, "What is this joint, anyway?"

In a quiet, exasperated whisper she replied, "Don't show your ignorance, Norman. This is a nightclub."

Well, I hadn't been in one before and I asked, "Do you suppose I can get a sermon illustration here?"

"I have my doubts." But she was wrong.

After a while, a woman came out to sing. She broke every rule I thought was necessary to be a nightclub singer. She was about fifty and looked it. She had no makeup on whatsoever that I could see. She was as homely as a—well, she was homely. Her hair had no style. She wore no jewelry. She had on a simple black dress that sort of hung on her. Pretty drab description, I admit it. But when she started to sing (and she wasn't the greatest singer I had ever heard, either) she let her personality flow out. She was different; she was herself. She made a contribution to me. She taught me once again that God puts a personality in each human being and if we let it be itself, truly itself, it is a wonderful thing.

You know what we need in this country? We need more nonconformists. I would like to start a campaign to produce the greatest generation of nonconformists we've ever had. You might ask, "What do you want with nonconformists? We've got nonconformists."

I want a nonconformist who will outnonconform the nonconformists. We have those who are nonconformist against the Puritan tradition. But these people are now old-fashioned and outdated. We need a new generation of young people, and older people, too, who will be their own fine, good, honest, dedicated selves, who will be so different from the common herd that everyone will look at them in astonishment.

Do you know what people will say? "We want to be like them."

The second thing to remember is this: By the grace of God you can do tremendous things. It makes no difference how little training, money, or status you have to begin with. The great question is what you do with what little you have. I remember one of my classmates from Ohio Wesleyan University who spoke to me one Sunday morning after I had preached a sermon. He said, "Norman, I'm glad to be here this morning. I've been studying you and I just want to say you've done pretty well with what little you have." Well, at the moment that disturbed me, but afterward I realized it was sort of a compliment. Anyone can bring wonderful things out of himself.

It makes no difference how unfavorable your situation, how many hazards you meet, what adversities you encounter; you can do tremendous things with yourself. I know a lady who is blind physically, but she is not blind spiritually. In her blindness she has become one of the greatest experts on Mexican cookery in the United States. She once had me to dinner in her home in San Francisco and served a fourteen-course dinner, every one a masterpiece, and all prepared by her. Yet, people come around and tell me how hard life is. I have even said that myself. Of course life is hard; it is made that way. It is supposed to be difficult. But the great message is that you can be a new creature through

Jesus Christ, and no matter how many difficulties you must face, you can develop a wonderful life.

As I rode down Fifth Avenue, I happened to look up at the Empire State Building. This, in its day, was the greatest building in New York City and it still is a marvelous structure. My mind went back to a boy who lived far downtown in New York in devastating poverty. When his father died, friends of the family had to chip in to buy a cheap coffin. His mother worked ten hours a day in an umbrella factory and continued working far into the night at home. The boy was a loyal member of the Catholic Church. He joined a drama society in the church and got such a thrill out of acting that he decided to try public speaking. He did so well that at the age of thirty he was elected to the New York State Assembly. There they put him on the committee on forests; he had never seen a forest in his life. Then they put him on the committee on banking; he had never had a bank account up to that time. He was so discouraged trying to read the bills that came before him, which he couldn't understand, that he almost decided to quit.

I am talking about Alfred E. Smith, four times Governor of New York State, once Democratic candidate for President of the United States, the greatest authority of his time on New York State government. He was a solid citizen who believed in the American system of freedom under God. And he realized his dream of building the tallest building in the world, the Empire State Building. I once sat with him in that building and said, "Governor, you have had a great career. Tell me about it."

He smiled and replied, "My mother always believed in me. She said there was something in me that God would bring out if I allowed Him to do so."

The great American story is that any boy or girl, however humble his beginnings, no matter what his education or his race or his background, has built within him marvelous personal gifts. These gifts can be brought out if he works and realizes that God never made another human being exactly like him and that he can do anything he wants to do.

So, if you are not satisfied with your life right here and now, say to the Lord, "Lord, I thank You for making me different. Help me to be different. Help me to bring out of myself the great person that is within me." What God can make out of a person is astounding.

A man started coming to Marble Collegiate Church when I was still the minister there, and I had never seen a more mixed-up, defeated human being. But he kept coming and one day he found Someone there, that Someone who can change any individual. I repeat and underscore, *any* individual. And He changed this man. Here is a letter he wrote to me:

Dear Dr. Peale,

When we think of all the wonderful things that have happened to us since we started going to Marble Collegiate Church, it seems nothing but a miracle. When you realize that six years ago this month I was totally broke, thousands of dollars in debt, a complete physical wash-out, and had hardly a friend in the world because of my excessive drinking, you can see why I have to pinch myself sometimes to realize that my good fortune is not all a dream.

As you well know, alcohol was not the only problem I had six years ago. It has been said that I was the most negative person anybody ever met. Filled with gripes and all sorts of irritations, I was the most supercritical, impatient, cocky individual you could imagine.

Now, please don't think I have overcome all these things. I haven't. At times I become discouraged with my progress. I am one of those people who have to do a day-by-day job on myself, and this I do. Gradually, by trying to follow the teachings of Jesus, I am learning to control myself and be a little less critical. It is like being released from a prison. I never dreamed life could be so full and wonderful.

Do as this man did and you will say to yourself with gladness in your heart, "How good God is!" There is no one quite like you. Be that one person God made and walk ahead, with the light of God on your face, and experience joy; release happiness and power. "If any man be in Christ, he is a new creature: old things are passed away; behold, all things are become new."

In the long run, you determine what your life will be by your decisions. Your decisions, little and big—and you never know when a little one is a big one in its consequences—will add up to what you become.

THREE
How to Make Right Decisions

How do you get the wisdom to make right decisions? In James 1:5 we read, "If any of you lack wisdom, let him ask of God, that giveth to all men liberally." A person cannot make right decisions consistently, except by stepping up his wisdom and stepping down his stupidities. Dale Carnegie, who wrote the book *How to Win Friends and Influence People,* was a great friend of mine. He told me once that he thought he'd write a book entitled *Dumb Things I Have Done.* I told him the difference between him and me was that I'd have to write a whole series of books to encompass the subject.

In the long run, you determine what your life will be by your decisions. Your decisions, little and big—and you never know when a little one is a big one in its consequences—will add up to what you become. You can decide yourself into failure or into success, into mental turmoil or into mental peace, into unhappiness or into happiness. A man remarked to me, "Let's face it; life goes the way the ball bounces." I don't go for any such idea as that at all! There is a deeper reality. You and I can decide, to a large degree, which way the ball bounces. We can control the bouncing of the ball of life's circumstances and outcomes, as we learn the art of making right decisions.

And how do we learn it? I repeat: If any man lacks wisdom, let him ask of God (really ask, *believing*), because God is liberal, and it will be given him. Believe, really believe, that there is an answer for you, and that God will give you the wisdom to find that answer. People who have become great people are those who have discovered that God will guide in all the problems of their lives. They have discovered that they can know God's guidance. This is no theory. I have seen it work in practice so many times that I could summon hundreds of witnesses to corroborate it. Let me call up two:

Some years ago, I had a pleasant friendship with the founder of the Kraft Foods Company, Mr. J. L. Kraft. He was a dedicated Christian, a great Baptist layman. He really loved the Lord Jesus Christ, and he had a tremendously astute mind. He was a truly remarkable individual with a simple but wise faith. One time, I got to talking with him about his early days.

Like many Americans, in the great tradition that has been a wonder to the world, Mr. Kraft started at the bottom. All he had was an old wagon, a horse called Paddy, and an idea about cheese processing. With his horse and wagon, he peddled his own cheese. Then he got two or three helpers. He told me he was always on the brink of failure in those early days. He said, "I would go home at night not knowing where I was going to get the money to pay my employees or to buy the materials I needed. But I always talked to God about it. I told God what I needed and asked Him for the wisdom to build up this business, so that I could do a service for Him in the world. And," he said, "God always heard me. God built my business."

He soon noticed, he said, that if he thought he had to have an answer to a problem by, say, nine o'clock Thursday morning, God might not give him the answer on Monday, or on Tuesday, or on Wednesday. But, if he really did have to have it at nine o'clock on Thursday morning, he then had the answer. And, if he didn't get it at nine o'clock Thursday, he would find out later he didn't need to have it then. When he did need it, he got it.

Mr. Kraft held the principle that if you need wisdom and you ask for it, and believe that there is an answer, it will come. He was one of the strongest personalities I ever knew because of his absolute, unshakable conviction that there was an answer and that God would give it to him. "Things didn't always turn out right," he noted, looking back on his career. "That was because I never was able to get rid of quite all the error in me. But to the degree to which you live with God, to that degree does error drop out and truth remain."

I have seen this demonstrated in some remarkable ways. For example, one night in Chicago I boarded a plane to go to Minneapolis, which is not a long flight. When we were airborne, the attendant sat down beside me and said she had a problem she would like to discuss. I said, "It had better be a little problem, because before you know it we'll be in Minneapolis."

"Well," she said, "it's a big problem to me. It's this: I've been dating two young men. They both tell me they're in love with me and want to marry me. The problem is, I don't know which one to take." She told me about the two young men and how she felt about each one—or thought she did. "Which one would you say I'm in love with?" she asked.

"Now look, this is not exactly in my line. Why don't you write to Dear Abby?"

"Because I've got you right here, Dr. Peale, and this problem really bothers me."

"Well, you've asked me, so I'll tell you. I don't think you love either. I wouldn't marry either one."

"But," she exclaimed, "I've got to marry one of them! I'm twenty-two years old!"

"Oh," I said, "don't let being twenty-two bother you. I still have an eye for feminine beauty, and I think you'll find someone. If you don't, they're all blind."

"You think I'll find the right one?" she asked anxiously.

"If you go at it the right way," I replied.

"What is the right way?"

"First," I said, "you must have a clear idea of just what kind of man you want. Make it specific. Can you describe the man you want to marry?"

"I want him to be nice looking," she said.

"To equate with your own looks, he would have to be. What else?"

Her face grew serious. "I want him to be a good man, a clean, decent person. And I hope there will be a lot of fun in him. Also, I want him to be a man who believes in God."

"Sister, you're all right," I said. "You've got a head on your shoulders. Now, what you should do is take that picture and hold it up to God, and just believe that you and that man will be drawn together in God's good time. But let's face it," I added, "maybe the man God brings you won't be handsome. Remember, the homely ones often turn out a lot better than the glamour boys. So don't press the Lord on that good-looking business. Be willing to settle for the answer you get from Him."

"I never thought of praying about a thing like this."

"Well," I asked, "aren't we supposed to pray about important things? And what could be more important than your lifelong companion, who will also be the father of your children? Isn't that something big enough to pray about?"

Often, we think of Christianity primarily as giving morality, or as giving sustaining strength in sickness or trouble. . . . But it also makes people wise.

Then I really went all out. I said, "Every day, as you stand at the top of the steps of your plane, I want you to visualize that sometime the perfect man for you will walk up those steps and right into your life!"

"Oh," she said, "do you think he will?"

"Why not? In any case, you'll meet him someplace."

And she did! He didn't walk up the steps of her plane, however. She met him at a church party while spending the weekend with her parents. "You know, it's wonderful the way things work out," she wrote to me. "The minute I saw him, I knew he was the one. He didn't know it—then. But it wasn't long before I got through to him and he knew it, too."

Everyone has a problem. And there is an answer to that problem. There is an answer to yours. So believe in that answer. Confide your desires to God, but be willing to take what He gives you. Believe that He will give you wisdom.

Often, we think of Christianity primarily as giving morality, or as giving sustaining strength in sickness or trouble. And it does give moral strength; it does give comfort, and peace, and love. But it also makes people wise. The more you live it, the more you have in you the mind that was in Christ Jesus our Lord. And you develop perceptiveness, astuteness, understanding, so that you have the wisdom out of which come right decisions. We can be healed of stupidity; we can be healed of dishonesty; we can also be healed of ineptitude. The second thing is to bear in mind that you never arrive at a truly wise decision unless it is a right decision. A wrong decision cannot turn out right, because it is wrong. Only a decision based on ethical rightness can be a wise decision. You may use some clever formula and get a clever result for the time being, but it won't hold if it has error in it. So be sure your decision is basically right.

J. Arthur Rank, the great British producer of motion pictures, who was also a devout Christian, held, they say, that the first principle of a decision is to consider, Is it right or is it wrong? It was said that often when Mr. Rank was with his associates and they were considering some problem, though he might be surrounded by fifteen or twenty men in a room, he would go into what he called "the silences." He had a remarkable ability to isolate himself behind a barrier of silence, even in the midst of confusion. And, in these silences, he would ask himself these questions: *Is this decision we are about to make a right one or a wrong one? Is there anything wrong about it, however small? It doesn't make any difference whether the amount involved is six thousand pounds or sixpence. The decision won't turn out right unless it is right.*

There are a lot of people in this world having trouble with decisions they have made, because they made them knowing there was wrongness in them. Most people know when a thing is wrong and when it is right. They may contend that they don't know. They sometimes maintain that there is a big gray area between the two, and you can't always tell what is right and what is wrong. I deny that. Wrong is wrong! You can squeeze it, and try to get the black out of it, and make it gray, until it almost gets to the edge of white, but it never quite does get white. It still has too much gray in it, which means basically it has too much black in it. Right is right and wrong is wrong!

This country, incidentally, grew great by following this principle. When I went to school, we knew right from wrong, because we had people teaching us who knew, and we had a culture in this country that knew. That was before we had characters like the present-day publishers of pornographic literature and other such people who have undercut the American concept of ethical values. But anyone who really seeks the truth still knows what is right and what is wrong. If he doesn't, then he'd better ask the Lord for wisdom, because when you admit an unethical factor into a decision, you get unethical and unfortunate results: The thing isn't soundly based and it won't hold up; it will let you down badly just when you can't afford it.

A friend asked if I would stop by and talk with him at his office. He said he wanted me to help him with a business decision. Knowing what business he was in and that I knew not the slightest thing about it, I remarked, "Bill, I don't know anything about your business. Why do you want me for a business decision?"

"You know about God's business, don't you?"

"A little," I replied.

"Well," he said, "this is God's business. Come on down. I'd come to you, but I've got a lot of papers and charts on this matter that I want you to see."

When I sat down with him in his office, and he started describing his problem, he used so many tabulations and diagrams that I was lost. I found myself mumbling at intervals, "Yes, I see. I see." Actually, all I saw was an isolated fact here and there. Then Bill produced a sheet of paper with a tentative solution outlined and a list of pros and cons lined up in two columns. "Please take a look at this," he said.

I read it through carefully but still had no grasp of the total problem. "Look, Bill," I said, "I know less than nothing about this technical problem. But one thing I can do is pray that you get the right insights and guidance."

"I'd like to go one better," he replied. "We'll pray together. But first let's have a few moments of mind-emptying. I know I'll never get the proper answer unless I first get all preconceived notions out of my mind. And two empty minds will be even better than one!" So we sat there trying to get our minds blank. Bill then prayed aloud: "Lord, our minds are emptied. Please fill them with truth about this situation. I don't want to make a mistake. Show me the right answer. Or show it to Norman, so he can show me."

We sat for another five minutes in silent prayer and reflection. Then suddenly, I remembered something I'd seen in one of the columns on that sheet of paper. I said, "Let me look at those columns again, Bill—those pros and cons." He showed them to me. I said, "Now, Bill, I don't know anything about it and it's all pretty involved, but this one point here bothers me. If you'll forgive my saying so, it looks a little shady." And I handed the sheet back to him, pointing to the item I meant.

Bill stared. "Well!" he exclaimed. "Here you are, knowing nothing about my business, yet when we emptied our minds and prayed, you put your finger on the very thing that has been troubling me the most! Now, surely you wouldn't spot it by your own intelligence alone." Which was certainly a fact, and I knew that better than he did! "This must be spiritual guidance," he added. "It just has to be. And it proves to me that this item has to be changed. Privately, I've been trying to convince myself it was not unethical and really no one's affair but mine. It would mean a little extra money for me, you see, if I let it stand. But I've been kidding myself. So out it comes. And now we've got a decision that is absolutely clean."

And, as the results later demonstrated, it did seem he'd had the benefit of more than his own wisdom, for the amended answer (minus the shady item) worked out beneficially for him and everyone concerned. God's guidance is always available.

Our lives today are the result of the decisions we have made over twenty years, thirty years, sixty years, as the case may be.

What is your life going to be five years from now? The decisions you make in the next five years will determine that. Remember, you can decide yourself into failure, confusion, or unhappiness, but he who humbly admits that he lacks wisdom can find it if he turns to God, who gives liberally. If you really ask Him, believing, God will fill you with perceptive understanding, reduce the error, and enhance the rightness, so that you will make right decision after right decision, and your life will be right. And when it's right, it's good and creative and joyous.

FOUR
GIVE THANKS—EVERY DAY

Thanksgiving is one of the most important, most creative capacities of the human mind. As we practice it, assiduously and constantly, we develop a deep joy in living, even though life is filled with all manner of suffering and difficulty.

The individual who learns to practice thanksgiving activates within himself, and around himself, continuous victories and blessings from God. If you practice thanksgiving, victory, and joy, satisfaction will be engendered in your life and will contribute to the happiness of all those who touch your life.

The idea of systematically practicing thanksgiving is hardly original with me. Actually it came to me from a man who regularly attended Marble Collegiate Church in the latter years of his life. His name was John Riley. At the time of his death, he was the oldest practicing physician in the state of New York. So long had he lived and practiced medicine that he had actually been, at one time, physician to President Grover Cleveland. He had also attended to President William Howard Taft on several occasions. And he was what you might call a character.

Sometimes, when we use the expression "he's a character," it carries a deprecatory connotation. To my notion, "a character" is an individual who is different—and Doctor Riley certainly was that. On his deathbed, he sent me a message. He said, "I'm dying, and I want you to send a message to Dr. Peale. Tell him to talk spiritually to the people, and I will be working for him on the other side." It touched me deeply that he would think of me as he went through the valley of the shadow of death, and his message was a source of encouragement.

One day, as he was chatting with me in my study, Dr. Riley had talked about this idea: If a person would each day deliberately practice thanksgiving, he would thereby activate new sources of energy and power within him. He stood up before me, straight and tall—a very alive and obviously healthy man, even in his nineties—and said, "Every day of my life, when I rise in the morning, I do my exercises and my deep breathing, and then I have a prayer and give thanks to God for my good body.

"The body," he continued, "is a wonderful instrument. Think of the skill that went into the making of its intricate, interrelated parts and functions! When it works well, it is a thing of beauty and a joy forever. And, one of the ways to make it work well is to affirm it as efficient.

"So," he said, "I start at my head and I run down through my whole body: I give thanks to God for my two eyes that

> *Do not be unmindful of the simple everyday
> blessings God showers upon you. The practice of the
> art of thanksgiving produces joy and satisfaction.*

bring the world into my awareness. I thank God for my
good digestion. I thank God for my joints, that they work
freely and without inhibition. I thank God for the temple of
the soul, and for the effectiveness of its operation over these
many years."

I stood looking at this man over ninety years of age, the
picture of health, and had a new sense of respect for the
physical body, temple of the soul, created by the good God.

The body is one of those things nearest to us that we tend
to take for granted, or that we disregard to our hurt. It
should be an object of thanksgiving.

Remember Psalm 103:2: "Bless the Lord, O my soul,
and forget not all his benefits." Do not be unmindful of the
simple everyday blessings God showers upon you. The practice of the art of thanksgiving produces joy and satisfaction.
I'm afraid most of us are deficient in the practice of thanksgiving, except on rare occasions. I've observed, however,
that the people who live the most joyously live in what you
might call a constant attitude of gratitude. They are astonished and delighted and receive the blessings of life with a
sense of wonder.

One such person I have known in my life was William L. Stidger. He was, in his time, one of the most distinctive and persuasive preachers in this country. He was a professor of theology and, as that usually implies, a great scholar; yet he also had, to a marked degree, that quality known as the human touch.

At one time, Bill Stidger had a nervous breakdown, during which he sat for months in abysmal gloom and mental darkness. I remember the description he gave me of this nervous breakdown. He said, "I cared nothing about anything. Everything was hopeless, everything was dark, everything was black—utter despondency."

And how do you think he emerged from this? By the practice of thanksgiving. One day, a friend told him that, with God's help, he could bring himself out of his despondency by practicing thanksgiving. And this friend suggested the manner in which he might go about it. "Think," he said, "of people who have greatly benefited you in your life, and ask yourself whether you have ever thanked them."

"I can think of many right away, but I do not recall having ever thanked one of them," Stidger said.

"Well," his friend suggested, "why don't you select one of them and write that person an affectionate letter of thanks?"

Stidger gave it some thought, and he remembered an old schoolteacher. Let us call her Miss Smith. He hadn't communicated with her in years, but he began to think about her. He remembered the gift she had of being able to inspire. It was she who had given him an appreciation of literature and made him love the great poets. (I never knew a man who could recite quite as much poetry—deeply meaningful poetry.) So he sat down and wrote her a letter, telling her that her influence had been a great blessing to him and that he had never forgotten her. He wrote that he wanted to thank her for what she had done for him.

He received, in reply, a letter written in the shaky handwriting of an aged lady. "Dear Willy," she wrote, addressing him by the nickname used in his boyhood. "When I read your letter, I was blinded with tears, for I remember you as a boy and, as I think of you now, I see you as a little fellow in my class. You have warmed my old heart." She continued, "I taught school for fifty years. Yours is the first letter of thanks I have ever received from a student, and I shall cherish it until I die."

This brought a ray of sunshine into Stidger's mind and encouraged him to try another letter of appreciation, and another, and another, until he had written five hundred such letters! In the years that followed, whenever depression began to seize him, he would take out his copies of the letters of thanks he had written to people, and the happiness he had experienced in writing them would well up in his heart once again.

This is a scientific procedure for anyone who wishes to develop joy and satisfaction in his life. "Bless the Lord, O my soul." Forget not all the benefits you have received from Him and from His children along life's way. If you're a bit down and discouraged right now, why not thank God, and then think of some human being to thank. Call that person on the phone, or send a telegram, or at least write a letter to express your thankfulness. Tell your wife how much you appreciate her, for example. She'll probably be so surprised she'll give you *two* slices of pie with your dinner.

Another way to practice thanksgiving is to remember what a wonderful country we live in, and give thanks for that. We need to be thankful for America. I really believe that if we Americans thanked God each day for what this country is, we would remember where its greatness came from and would learn how to keep it great.

The problem of preserving our country is acute. We do not realize how easily a civilization can decay. I have been to Byblos, at the eastern end of the Mediterranean Sea, where you can see, at a glance, the excavated traces of seven successive civilizations, due to the skill with which the excavations there have been performed: Egyptian, Phoenician, Persian, Greek, Roman, and others. All mighty civilizations. If, at the height of any of those civilizations, a preacher had stood in a pulpit and said, "This civilization can die," his listeners would have laughed at him. But they all did die, and their cities were covered over by dirt and sand, and now a few crumbling monuments are all that is left of them. This mighty civilization of ours likewise has within it the seeds of death. All human beings have within them the seeds of death. You have them. I have them. It is necessary to counteract these seeds of death with those of life. Our civilization can die, or our civilization can live.

Edward Gibbon, eighteenth-century author, in his classic

Decline and Fall of the Roman Empire, cites several causes for the deterioration of Roman power. The prevalence of divorce and breakdown of the home was one. Building up vast armaments was another. Enormous taxes that drained all incentive from the worker was another. Spending vast sums of money for bread and circuses, to entertain the populace and blind them to the decay of their political institutions, was another. Do these things sound familiar? In our thankfulness for our wonderful country, we should remember that its civilization was given to us by God.

This nation was originally established on a definitely religious base. I have copied down, for example, the beginning of the Mayflower Compact. Now, the men and women who came to this continent in the *Mayflower* were tough-minded believers in God, and they didn't accommodate themselves to everyone else's beliefs so that everyone would be nice to everyone else. They had convictions and principles. Nowadays, we are so afraid we are going to offend someone's sensibilities that everything is getting reduced to the lowest common denominator—with emphasis on the word "lowest." Here is what those who prepared the Mayflower Compact wrote first: "In the name of God, amen." That is the way the whole business began. "In the name of God, amen." There are lots of people today who wouldn't do it that way. They would work up something like this: "In the name of philosophical interfaith harmony, in which we are all brothers and all avoid voicing opinions to which anyone might take exception . . ." and so forth.

The Mayflower Compact then declares:

We whose names are under-written, the loyal subjects of our dread Sovereign Lord King James by the Grace of God of Great Britain, France, Ireland, King, Defender of the Faith. . . . Having undertaken, for the glory of God and advancement of the Christian Faith [they never could say that today] and honor of our King and country, a voyage to plant the first colony in the northern parts of Virginia, do by these presents solemnly and mutually in the presence of God and one of another, covenant and combine ourselves together into a civil body politic. . . .

Is that old-fashioned? Have we gotten beyond it? Well, that is the way America began; that is what made it great.

When they got around to the New England Confederation, they wrote: "But all came into this part of America with one and the same purpose to advance the Kingdom of our Lord Jesus Christ and to enjoy the liberties of the Gospel." How things have changed! For example, one of the most eminent divinity schools in the United States used to have on all its literature, and in its buildings, the motto *Christo et Ecclesia*—"for Christ and the Church." This phrase was later eliminated from the catalogs because it represented too narrow a point of view. Apparently, that divinity school doesn't go 100 percent for Jesus Christ. It practices accommodation.

Now, maybe the school could offer some justification. But weak, willy-nilly behavior of this kind can never produce, or maintain, a great nation. As the outward emphasis on God has decreased, so have ethics and morals come to a sad condition—so much so that a Chief Justice of the United States not long ago made a speech on how urgently we need to recover ethics and morals.

I was reading an editorial in the *Wall Street Journal*, a paper that runs some of the finest editorials I come across anywhere in American newspapers. This editorial gave quite an extensive treatment to the Chief Justice's speech on ethics and morals, the gist of which seemed to be that we no longer know what is moral or what is ethical. Consequently, legal associations and business associations develop codes of ethics for their own observance: "This is ethical; that is not ethical."

Where did we originally get our ethics? Right out of the Bible. But now we have come to a point where many people believe that the ethics of the Bible are narrow or old-fashioned. So, for new ethics, they look to professors who develop them out of their personal prejudices or viewpoints. I, for one, am not about to let any professor in the United States substitute his morals and ethics for those taught in the Bible.

Are we going to become so liberal that we abandon the ethical and moral principles on which this nation was established? Do we or don't we believe in the ethics and the morality of the Bible? If we do—we who are Christians—then we should be committed and dedicated, thanking God for the goodness He gave to us through His Son, Jesus Christ, and for the benefits that have accrued therefrom.

The Chief Justice went on to observe that the home no

longer teaches religion. And now that religion is completely taken out of the educational process, who, he asked, is going to teach us ethics? Let us thank God that there are still people who are reaching out for God to bring Him back into our lives today.

In conclusion, I would like to quote from a statement by Carlos P. Romulo, the Philippine statesman who served long at the UN, playing an important part in its development—a great, solid thinker.

General Romulo, before returning home to the Philippines to become president of the University of the Philippines, wrote this moving farewell to America:

> I am going home, America—farewell.
>
> For 17 years, I have enjoyed your hospitality, visited every one of your 50 states. I can say I know you well.
>
> I admire and love America. It is my second home.
>
> What I have to say to you, now, in parting, is both a tribute and a warning: *Never forget, Americans, that yours is a spiritual country.*
>
> Yes, I know that you are a practical people. Like others, I have marveled at your factories, your skyscrapers, and your arsenals.
>
> But, underlying everything else is the fact that America began as a God-loving, God-fearing, God-worshiping people, knowing that there is a spark of the Divine in each one of us. It is this respect for the dignity of the human spirit which makes America invincible. May it always endure.
>
> And, so I say again, in parting, thank you, America,

and farewell. May God keep you always—and may you always keep God.

Each day, let us bless the Lord and be mindful of all He has done for us, as individuals and as a nation. Let us keep God.

FIVE

THE MAGIC OF BELIEVING

The mail received by ministers is sometimes most extraordinary. People are likely to write to us about the most intimate concerns of their lives. The subject matter may cover the gamut of human experience: from drama to tragedy, with comedy in between. I once received the following letter from a Baptist minister in California:

> I came across an interesting story the other day— about a young man who liked to play the horses. At a local store, he came upon a book entitled *You Can Win* and, thinking it was a tip sheet, he purchased it. Imagine his surprise when he discovered at the racetrack that it was a book by Norman Vincent Peale on how to win in the game of life! He tells me he didn't have any winning horses that day, but it was the luckiest day he ever had—because through that book he came to know Jesus Christ as his Savior.

You see, you never know where—or how—the simple message of the Gospel is going to reach a person. That

> *Believing . . . is hard. It requires mental discipline. It requires self-surrender. It requires giving your whole self to it.*

young man got it when his attention was diverted from horse racing to a book about the magic of believing. His betting on the horses did not pay off, but the magic of believing, if he continues to pursue it, will pay off in dividends beyond compare through all the days of his life. Indeed, whoever applies the magic of believing to his problems, and to his life, will have wonderful results.

There is a text in the New Testament bearing on this point: Mark 9:23. It is probably one of the greatest gems of truth you will find in the greatest Book of wisdom in the world: "If thou canst believe, all things are possible to him that believeth." Notice that you are offered something tremendous, but there's an *if.* "*If* thou canst believe," then all things are possible. Believing—in the depth to which we are now directing our thought—is hard. It requires mental discipline. It requires self-surrender. It requires giving your whole self to it. It isn't something off the top, or the surface, of your mind. It certainly isn't the glib recital of a creed. But, if you can overcome your doubts and your negativisms and really, deeply believe, you will thereby enter into a life transformed, for "all things are possible to him that believeth." This is the magic of believing.

Belief is factual; it is truth. The term *magic* is synonymous with utter wonder. The magic of believing is a manifestation of one of the greatest powers in the universe, the power of thought. By our thoughts, we either create or destroy.

You can build up your life by thinking constructively. You can tear down your life by destructive thinking. What you are this day is the result of what you have been thinking for many years. We become what we think. If you would like to know what you will be, let us say, five years from now, you do not need any soothsayer or fortune-teller to give you the facts. I can give them to you right this minute. Five years from now, you will be precisely what you think over the next five years. You will be a bigger person, then, if you think big; you will be a smaller person if you think small. We do not bear in mind nearly enough the creative and the destructive power of thought. The Roman Marcus Aurelius wrote, "Our life is what our thoughts make it." Emerson said that a man is what he thinks about all day.

Now, thought isn't something that is ethereal. A thought is actually a thing. It has substance. A thought is also alive. "Cut a word," said Emerson, "and it will bleed." That is a picturesque way of saying that a thought is alive. Emerson doesn't mean that literal drops of blood are going to come out of the word. But he is saying that, if you take a word that is vital and put it with some other vital words to make a thought, it can cause life or deterioration, according to the manner in which you use it.

Suppose, for example, you are a negative thinker. You are

full of negative thoughts from morning until night, and you voice them. What are you doing? Something dangerous: you are activating negatives in the world around you. There is a law that like attracts like. If you send out negative thoughts, you activate negative influences in the world through the operation of this law of attraction, and you draw back to yourself negative results. There is no other way it could be. On the other hand, if you send out positive thoughts—bright, resplendent thoughts of faith—you activate positive influences in the world around you, and you draw back to yourself positive results.

Let's suppose you think fear thoughts. These thoughts activate fearsome anxious tendencies in the life around you, and you draw back anxiety results to yourself. If, on the other hand, you remind yourself, "I am a child of God, and God is with me, so I need not be afraid," you will be sending out positive thoughts of courage and faith, and if you keep it up, you will draw back to yourself thoughts of courage and faith. We get what we think. The magic of believing brings back to us the great things a good God gives.

I was in Charlottesville, Virginia, sometime ago. In front of the hotel in Charlottesville is a marvelous statue of the famous Confederate General Stonewall Jackson, who was in some respects one of the greatest men this country produced. Once, when Stonewall Jackson was planning an audacious Civil War campaign in the Shenandoah Valley, a timorous general—one of his subordinate commanders—came to him the night before a scheduled forward push. He said, "General, I'm afraid. I'm afraid that this is an improper deployment of our troops. I'm afraid our strategy is not sound. I fear we're going to lose a lot of men."

The great Jackson put his hand on the shoulder of this commander and said, "General, never take counsel of your fears."

If you take counsel of your fears, your fears will reproduce themselves. If you harbor doubts about yourself and your ability, and think of yourself as inferior, you will get back failures and limitations. It is very serious, friends, how we so often defeat ourselves by our thoughts, when by the magic of believing, we could be winning victories.

Years ago, I read a statement by the late American psychiatrist Karl Menninger that fascinated me. A man who had heard me quote this statement in a sermon once presented me with a wooden plaque with the words inscribed on it, and I keep that plaque in my study. I've had people come in, look at it, and want to argue about it. And I've had others come in and be inspired by it. This is what the plaque says: "Attitudes are more important than facts."

You will sometimes hear hardheaded businesspeople stressing the point that facts are facts. And some people have the notion that nothing is more important than facts. But it just isn't so. The most important thing is not the facts but your attitude toward the facts.

One man examines a situation and says, "Well, those are the facts. There's nothing you can do about it. The only thing you can do is accept the facts." That is his attitude toward the facts—so the facts defeat him. Another man looks at the situation and says, "Those are the facts, all right. But I never saw a set of facts yet to which there wasn't a solution. Some facts can be changed. And where there is one that can't be changed, maybe I can get around it, or under it, or over it. Or, maybe I can weave that fact into a new pattern and live with it and use it to my advantage." His attitude toward the facts brings the magic of believing into play, and he defeats the facts rather than letting the facts defeat him. "If thou canst believe. . . ." If you can only believe, then nothing shall be impossible to you.

One time, when I was speaking at a business convention, I spoke along this line—which is a theme I often touch upon, because I think it points the way to living victoriously. After my speech, a man came up to me and said, rather wistfully, I thought, "I only wish I could believe all that you said about the power of believing."

"Well," I told him, "one way is to practice believing it. And I would suggest you study the passages on faith in the Bible. It's the Bible that tells us, 'All things are possible to him that believeth.' "

"Where is that?" he asked, and I told him he would find it in Mark 9:23. Then he protested, "But, you just don't know my problems. I've got a lot of trouble. Being a preacher, you wouldn't understand that."

"Say that again, my friend."

"I've got a lot of trouble," he repeated.

I assured him that I shared his feelings about trouble but said that, when I feel I am having a hard time, I often think of a line from an old spiritual: "Nobody knows the trouble

I've seen. Glory Hallelujah!" Yes, we have trouble, but we also have God. So, Glory Hallelujah! With faith in God we can overcome the trouble.

I finally convinced him to give the magic of believing a try. And what do you think he did? Like many other executives, he was accustomed to having boxes on his desk for the mail, reports, and papers he must deal with. There was a box for incoming items, one for the outgoing mail, and a third labeled "Undecided." The "Undecided" box usually had more in it than the other two boxes put together. But now, he got a fourth box and put it alongside the other three. He put a label on it that said, "With God All Things Are Possible." When he found himself faced with a tough problem, he'd write a memo on it and throw the memo and any related papers into this fourth box. There he would leave the matter, believing that, when the problem had to have an answer, God would supply it. He would pray about the situation and surround it with the magic of believing. Some weeks later, he wrote, "It's wonderful, the results I get from this box." This may be a simple, primary-school way to do business. But it demonstrates that believing brings results.

A distinguished Canadian chemist wrote a book I have kept at my bedside for years. It is called *Let Go and Let God*. You wouldn't think a distinguished chemist would write a book on this subject, would you? But this one did. He was the late Albert E. Cliffe. He was a food chemist, one of the greatest in Canada. He was also a religious man and conducted a large Bible class in Toronto. "As a chemist," he wrote, "I have faith in science, and I can prove it every day. The salt we use so commonly is made up of two deadly poisons; combined in a certain manner, they produce a commodity which is absolutely essential for every one of us. This is the magic of believing the laws of chemistry." He summed up his views on believing by saying he was no theologian and had no desire to study orthodox theology in any university. "I simply believe that God is my Father and that I am His son, and that my mind is a part of His Divine mind—and by this magic of believing I can be in tune with that tremendous mind of His at any time I choose. And, by so doing and by so believing, I can gain the answer to any problem which I have to face."

He goes on to say:

What you get out of religion is entirely up to you. You can make your faith a super atomic dynamo, or you can make it a routine affair without progress. You can be healed right now, and your healing can start at any time, regardless of how serious your condition may appear to you, if you will let go your fears and give God His rightful place in your life.

How can you afford to refuse this man, Jesus Christ, when you see every day in your life what faith in Him can produce? This Christ became a reality to me many years ago; and the freedom from pain, from sickness, and from fear, which I have had in these intervening years, is what I am trying to offer you through the medium of these words today. What He has done for me, what He has given me, He is willing to give you, if you will try to practice the magic of faith, the magic of believing.

On the authority of the Bible and of human experience, no matter what your problem may be, or your difficulty, or your defeat, there is enough power in the magic of believing to overcome any or all of it *"if* thou canst believe." And you *can* believe, if you will surrender your life to Him. The magic of believing stimulates a wonderful flow of power. Christianity is a fount of power—of the greatest power in the universe. The Bible is a Book of power that contains techniques of power and formulas of power. Jesus, after His resurrection, said to the disciples, "You shall receive power when the Holy Spirit has come upon you" (*see* Acts 1:8). That was the beginning of the Christian faith: a promise of power.

How much power have you? Are you living on a great flow of power, or are you livng on a miserable little trickle? Do you have a great surging of power, or do you have just a little rivulet that carries you through some things but fails you in others? The law of supply is a great concept, and this law of supply is offered to anyone who will practice the magic of believing.

This doesn't mean you are going to get rich. Christianity isn't designed to make you rich; Christianity isn't interested in whether or not you are rich. The Bible says, "Cast thy bread upon the waters: for thou shalt find it after many days" (Ecclesiastes 11:1). You shall have every one of your needs satisfied, if you practice the magic of believing.

Sometime ago, I heard of a furniture manufacturer in Grand Rapids, Michigan, who learned this lesson.

The basic spiritual law of the universe, demonstrated by Jesus Christ, who gave His life, is that blessings come from giving yourself away.

This man, using the ordinary procedures of business, got into difficulties and almost went broke. He was able to save the factory, but his credit was thin. The bankers wouldn't loan him money. However, he had a few friends who, out of sentiment, loaned him enough to get started again. But he said to himself, "Somehow or other, things elude me. I haven't got what it takes to do a successful job. I'm failing at some point."

Then he began to pray and read the Bible, and he got the idea of tithing—giving ten percent of his income and his time to the Lord. So, when he was ready to start his factory on a thin line of credit, he went to his office and knelt down and said to the Lord, "Lord, this plant, such as it is, is Yours. I accept You now as my partner and I will give the first ten percent, all the rest of my life, to You."

He began to make furniture again, and he kept giving part of his money away. As he gave, more money came back to him. Then his credit got better because his results were better, and the bankers began to loan him money. They were puzzled because part of the money they loaned him he used in his business, but part of it he gave away. They said, "That isn't practical." But his business grew, and he brought blessings to other people.

As you give, you gain—not only monetarily but in all of the more precious blessings of life as well. The basic spiritual law of the universe, demonstrated by Jesus Christ, who gave His life, is that blessings come from giving yourself away. Can you believe this? Have you got what it takes to believe it? If you can believe this, all things are possible.

Try it!

SIX

FILL YOUR HEART WITH HOPE

"Hope springs eternal in the human breast." And it is well that it does, for we cannot live without hope. With it, we can live successfully. It doesn't make any difference how much difficulty people experience; with hope, they can still go forward.

Hope! What a wonderful word it is! Write it indelibly on your mind. H-O-P-E. It is a bright word, shining and scintillating and dynamic, forward-looking, full of courage and optimism. With this word, let us begin tomorrow.

What lies beyond the threshold of today you do not know, nor do I. We can speculate, but we do not know. Inescapably, however, we must cross that threshold and, with the golden gift of hope, we can cross confidently, eagerly, optimistically.

Looking over a list of twenty-five persons who had written to me asking for prayers, I saw requests from Pennsylvania, North Carolina, Michigan, Illinois, Tennessee, Mississippi, California, Maryland, Arkansas, Florida, Indiana, and Ohio.

> *We have . . . three words:* faith, hope, *and*
> love. *Have that trinity in your mind, live by*
> *those shining words, and you have the secret*
> *of human life and life eternal.*

Lest you have any doubts about how much people need hope, let me recite at random from that list some of the situations for which people were asking prayers. "Diabetes" . . . "husband out of a job" . . . "daughter mentally ill" . . . "forty thousand dollars in debt" . . . "bedridden for thirty-eight years." There was a person on the list who had lost the senses of taste and smell; another whose son was in jail; and a woman who asked for prayers to help her overcome hate. There you are—a panorama of human problems!

Now, it is a function of the church of Jesus Christ to have a word for human desperation, human depression, human suffering, and woe. We have the word; or better still, three words: *faith, hope,* and *love.* Have that trinity in your mind, live by those shining words, and you have the secret of human life and life eternal. Faith, hope, and love. "Why art thou cast down, O my soul? and why art thou disquieted within me? hope thou in God: for I shall yet praise him, who is the health of my countenance, and my God" (Psalm

42:11). No matter what difficulties you may face, if you hope in God, the time will come when you will praise Him for your victory and for His goodness.

This life is not easy! It is often fraught with pain and suffering. But hope gives you a lilting upthrust that takes you above the suffering. Storms sweep down upon human beings individually. They sweep down over society. But if you hope in God and do the right thing, storms pass after a while.

No one ought to go through life without developing a philosophy about storms. Storms are to toughen wood; storms are to plow up the earth; storms are to test human beings; storms are hard, but one great thing about storms is that they always pass. And the things that are deeply rooted in the truth of Almighty God endure. So, if you are in harmony with God, you can have hope no matter how furious the storm.

I was once in Columbus, Ohio, to make a speech. I prevailed upon a friend to drive me to Lynchburg, a little town in the southern part of the state, some eighty-five miles from Columbus. I wanted to go to Lynchburg to visit my father's grave. After my father's passing, I ordered a gravestone, and I wanted to see for myself whether it was properly set. So, I found myself in the town where my mother and father grew up, where I had spent many a day as a boy. I went to the cemetery and communed with my father and mother. But it was not because they were there in the cemetery; that is the resting place of their bodies only. They themselves are not there. Neither are any of your loved ones in any grave.

After leaving the cemetery, I went up the street to the house that had been my grandparents' house. It had been sold to a woman named Grace Williams. Each time I visited Lynchburg, I would call and talk with Mrs. Williams. She was always kind to me. I grew fond of her, and I felt sad when she died.

I will never forget my first meeting with her. I went to the house. There was an old-fashioned bell in the door. You twirled it, and it made a musical sound. I twirled the bell, and a sweet-looking woman came to the door. I asked, "Are you Mrs. Williams?"

She replied, "Yes, and you're one of the Peales, aren't you?"

I said, "Yes."

"Which one are you, Norman or Robert?"

"I am Norman."

"Aha!" she said. "Do I know you! Your name is written all over my wallpaper. As a youngster, you apparently believed in advertising." From that day, we were wonderful friends.

During that first visit with Mrs. Williams, I told her that I was much attached to the old-fashioned doorbell, which I could remember twirling as a child. "It evokes memories," I said. Well, I had just arrived home a few days later when a package arrived. It was the bell. Mrs. Williams had taken it out of the door and sent it to me. I still have it, and every once in a while I twirl it and go back through the years in memory.

The last time I saw Mrs. Williams, we were standing on the porch, and I said, "I see the old tree is still there. It must be one hundred, maybe one hundred twenty-five years old."

"Yes," she said, "that is a great tree. I love it."

"So do I." And I remembered a night, years ago, when my brother Bob and I were small boys. My grandmother had just put us to bed when a terrible storm came up. We could hear the wind whirling around the house, making a deep, whistling sound as though it came out of the vortex itself. And then the flash of lightning, followed by a clap of thunder. The rain was hurled in great sheets against the windows. The house shook. Bob and I were scared and, from where I lay, I could see, silhouetted against the window, that great tree. Seeing how violently it was being tossed by the storm, I was suddenly filled with terror. I always have loved trees and I loved that one. I turned to Bob and cried, "That tree will never last this out. It will go down." We jumped out of bed and scurried downstairs to where my grandmother was sitting by a kerosene lamp. A dyed-in-the-wool Methodist, she was reading the *Christian Advocate*. We cried, "Grandma! Grandma!"

"What's the matter?" she asked calmly.

"The tree! It's going to go down."

Well, my grandmother was a wise Christian woman. She bundled us up and took us out on the porch in the wind and rain. She said, "Isn't it great to feel the rain on your face? Isn't it great to get out here in the wind? God is in the rain. God is in the wind. Just look at that tree. That tree is having a good time with the storm. It yields to it, bending one way or the other. It doesn't fight it. It cooperates with it. It is playing with the storm. It is laughing with the wind and the rain. I don't think it will go down. It will be there for a long time to come. Now, you go to bed, boys. God is in the storm, and all storms ultimately pass."

So we went back to bed. Storms come and go, but a great tree stands. It stands because it has driven its roots deep down into the earth. That is why it can grow high. That is how it rides out the storms.

When people crash under storms, when they have nervous breakdowns or go to pieces in some other way, they do not have the proper root system. Send down into the soil of your life the three great roots of faith, hope, and love, and nothing in this world can shake you, for you will be living in cooperation with Almighty God.

Shakespeare says, "The miserable have no other medicine, but only hope." He also says of hope, "It is a great and healing potion." Hope is a medicine that gives you power inwardly. When you have hope in your heart, you stand straighter, you throw back your shoulders, you breathe deeply of God's good air, and your mind is filled with healthy thoughts.

The primary function of counseling psychologists is to

help people clean their hearts and minds so they may have hope and thereby power.

I once received a letter from my mechanic, telling me my car was in bad shape. It needed to be fixed. On the enclosed card it said, "A clean engine always delivers power." Well, we had to have the valves ground and quite a lot of work done to get that engine clean. That is just as true of a human being as it is of an engine. Get the hate out of your mind, get the fear out of your mind, get the conflicts out of your mind, and hope will flow into it. Then you will have the power to live, for with hope come aliveness, enthusiasm, vibrancy, and vitality.

A friend of mine sent me a quotation from Elbert Hubbard, one of the greatest inspirational writers this country ever produced. He is worth reading. His writings glow with vitality. Here, from Elbert Hubbard, is a priceless piece of writing that is full of the hope and power with which we should live today:

Whenever you go out of doors, draw the chin in, carry the crown of the head high, and fill the lungs to the utmost; drink in the sunshine; greet your friends with a smile and put soul into every handclasp.

Do not fear being misunderstood and do not waste a minute thinking about your enemies. Try to fix firmly in your mind what you would like to do, and then, without veering of direction, you will move straight to the goal. Keep your mind on the great and splendid things you would like to do, and then, as the days go gliding by, you will find yourself unconsciously seizing upon the opportunities that are required for the fulfillment of your desire.

Picture in your mind the able, earnest, useful person you desire to be, and the thought you hold is hourly transforming you into that particular individual.

Thought is supreme. Preserve a right mental attitude—the attitude of courage, frankness, and good cheer. To think rightly is to create. All things come through desire and every sincere prayer is answered. We become like that on which our thoughts are fixed.

These words of Elbert Hubbard are as sound as the good earth on which we stand. How do they apply to you? What do you habitually think about yourself? Do you think of yourself as old and weary, or as sick or discouraged or gloomy? Do you think of yourself as having no ability? Do you think of yourself as defeated? Then, in the name of God, get some hope into your mind and change that thought pattern, for otherwise your living will be as negative as your thoughts.

So pull yourself up—physically, mentally, spiritually. Do it by filling your mind with the Bible and with hope. "Hope thou in God: for I shall yet praise him, who is the health of my countenance" (Psalm 42:11). As you hope in Him, trust in Him, serve Him, you will have health in your countenance because you will have health all through you— body, mind, and spirit.

Pull the fresh air into your lungs and hope into your

mind. Remember that you do not go into the world alone but with God, who has walked with you ever since you were a child; and that the Lord Jesus Christ is with you, too. Begin tomorrow with hope. Unlock the mysterious door of the future with the golden key of hope in God.

SEVEN

HEALED—BY THE GREAT PHYSICIAN

At intervals, I feel it is my duty as a Christian minister to deal with the subject of the healing power of faith. This isn't the easiest topic in the world to handle, and it was a long road by which I personally came to a complete belief in the healing power of faith. I was reared in a family of ministers and physicians and always took a rather coldly scientific view of the healing process. I abhorred anything that smacked of quackery. But some years ago, I had a profound experience that changed my attitude.

One night, I was awakened by the insistent ringing of the telephone. I snapped on the light, looked at my clock, and saw that it was 2:00 A.M. Picking up the telephone receiver, I heard the familiar voice of a close friend of mine, a leading physician in Syracuse, New York, where this experience took place. My friend apologized, "Norman, I'm sorry to awaken you, but I have a patient about whom I am greatly concerned. I cannot seem to bring about a crisis. I need help. Will you come and join me here?"

"What in the world could I do to help you, except pray?"

He rebuked me, "What could possibly be more powerful than prayer? Please come."

I went. But I was nervous. Before ringing the doorbell, I stopped and prayed and asked the Lord to guide my faltering efforts. The doctor admitted me. "My patient is very ill. What I want you to do is join me in filling this sickroom to overflowing with the healing power of Jesus Christ." You may think that is a strange way for a physician to talk, but it was not so strange. And this particular physician was a member of many learned societies, one of the most highly respected men of medicine of his time.

I looked at the woman in the bed. Her face was white. She seemed to me to be in a deep coma. I whispered, "What are her chances?"

"I've had consultations," he answered. "I've done all I can. It is now in the hands of the Great Physician. But," he said, "don't minimize Him. He has great power." He motioned me to a seat and took one himself on the other side of the bed. "Let us pray silently and in-depth for her, trying to drive our prayers into her consciousness."

Thus we prayed. I opened my eyes once and looked across at him. I told him later, "If, when I am dying, I can look up and see your face by my bed, I'll have confidence and serenity."

Then the doctor began to quote healing passages of Scripture and nodded to me to do the same. I did. Then he quoted more passages. It seemed as though they just welled up out of him, until we could sense Jesus Christ in that room. I started quoting passages of Scripture that I didn't feel I could remember in their entirety. For some strange reason, I found myself quoting them almost verbatim. They had been buried in my subconscious. My conscious mind didn't know them, but my subconscious mind did, and God gave them back to me.

This went on for some time. Finally, color began to come into the woman's cheeks. Then the most amazing thing happened: She opened her eyes wide, looked at us both, and then started to recite Scripture passages herself.

Later the doctor said to me, "The crisis has passed. She will sleep now. I'm sure she will get well." Which she did—and lived for many years thereafter.

As I left that house, my friend went to the door with me, commenting, "Jesus isn't dead, is He? He was in this house tonight." Neither of us could speak easily, we were so moved by His presence.

It was by now 5:00 A.M. Sleep was of no concern to me at all; I was so excited. I had never felt more alive, more awake, in my life. I could hardly contain myself. I remember that I walked for a long time, overwhelmed by the wonder and the glory and the majesty of it all, with a whole new consciousness of the power of God dawning in my mind: We heal through God's servants the doctors, and we also heal through our own faith.

I found myself remembering one of the most beautiful scenes described in the New Testament. Jesus was on a plain near the sea. A great multitude had gathered. Great multitudes always gather when He is present, because no one has ever been loved as He is loved. The Bible says, "And the whole multitude sought to touch him: for there went virtue out of him, and healed them all" (Luke 6:19). In the King James Version of the Bible, from which I have just quoted, the word *virtue* is often used in a larger sense, in which it means the power of goodness or, as one modern dictionary gives it, the "active quality of power." The Revised Standard Version renders this text: "For power came forth from him and healed them all."

The Bible also says that Jesus Christ is "the same yesterday, and to day, and for ever" (Hebrews 13:8). He has not lost His ancient skill. The multitudes still gather today; and I tell you, in His name, that if we really seek to touch Him, power will come out of Him and heal us all!

How does this healing power operate? It heals the body, but that is secondary. The real sickness of man is in his mind and in his soul. And this is the unity that Jesus Christ makes whole. When you are whole in soul, mind, and body, you live with power and joy.

A prominent Japanese physician with whom I am acquainted says he has found that physical disability, or illness, is often traceable to some disorder of mind, heart, or relationship with other people. "The disability," he says, "arises out of this disorder." This physician doesn't happen to be a Christian. He is a Japanese Buddhist. But he makes the statement that if some power could eliminate disorder from people's lives, their health quotient would be high indeed.

There is a physician in the Midwest who said, "If I can get people into the area of pure joy, even for one minute every day, I can keep them well." And what is this area of pure joy? "It is a perfect contact with Jesus Christ, the Great Physician," said the doctor. "There is healing in His touch." So, whatever disorder you have in your life, bring it to the Lord, and ask Him to straighten it out.

I have a book entitled *God Is Able* by a former New York City colleague, Dr. John Ellis Large, who was once rector of the Church of the Heavenly Rest on Fifth Avenue. Dr. Large had much experience in the healing ministry. He told about a man named George. This man's wife, Sarah, was one of Dr. Large's parishioners, although she never came to church or had anything to do with the religious life of the church, except when she got into trouble. One day she came to see him and said, "Dr. Large, I shouldn't take your time. I've been on your church rolls, but I'm what is commonly known as 'dead wood.' But," she said, "I have a real problem. It is my husband. My husband isn't well. He's irritable; he's irascible; he's full of tension; he's on edge all the time. He's a disappointed, frustrated, unhappy man. And he's developed all sorts of symptoms of poor physical health. He has gone to the doctor, and the doctor says there isn't anything really wrong with him that wouldn't be straightened out if he got his life in order.

"I've tried to talk to him about it," she continued, "but he just swears at me. It's difficult. He misses one promotion after another at the office. All the men he started out with in his company have moved ahead faster than he has. This fills him with indignation and resentment. I talked with his boss. He said, 'George is contentious; he is not cooperative;

he doesn't play ball; he has no enthusiasm; and he is full of meanness.' "

So Dr. Large suggested to this troubled wife, "Why don't you bring your husband to see me?"

"He would never come," she replied. "He has no use for you, or any minister, or for the church. I can't even get him to pray with me. He says he is fed up with God. He says he doubts there really is a God."

"Well, then," said Dr. Large, "let us give him some treatment at home." And he asked her this peculiar question: "What are your husband's sleeping habits?"

"He tosses most of the night," she said, "wears himself out groaning and moaning, but by five o'clock in the morning he is in a deep sleep. And I have to wake him up to get him to the office."

"All right," the rector said, "at five o'clock every morning, you get up and sit by your husband, and pray for him. Believe that Jesus Christ is there by your husband's side, actually present with you and with him. Imagine your husband as a whole man—happy, controlled, organized, and well. Hold that thought in your mind, for an image will become a fact as you hold it. Think of your prayers as reaching his unconscious. At that time in the morning, his conscious mind is not resisting and you can get an idea into his unconscious.

"Visualize him as kindly, cooperative, happy, creative, and enthusiastic."

"Why," she exclaimed, "I never heard anything like that before!"

"Well, it's time you heard it," he told her. "You go and do it."

She said, afterward, that she soon got so she didn't need an alarm clock. She would wake up promptly at 5:00 A.M. and hover over her husband in the company of Christ, projecting these thoughts and prayers into his unconscious. For many weeks, nothing seemed to happen. Finally, George said to her one day, "You know, it's strange how nice everybody has become—people I used to think were hating me and double-crossing me and everything. What's come over them? They're all so nice. Everything is so different."

Some days later, he came to her when he arrived home from work and said, "What do you know! The boss is making me a division manager. I asked him why in the world he would do that. And he said, 'Because of the great change in you. You're happy; you're cooperative; you play ball; you're enthusiastic—you're becoming one of the best men we have.' "

His wife never did tell him how he was reached. But the disorder left his life. The power of Jesus Christ is very skillful. "God moves in a mysterious way, His wonders to perform . . ." said the eighteenth-century poet William Cowper. No wonder the multitudes two thousand years ago sought to touch Him, and power came out of Him and healed them all! And today, twenty centuries later, He is still the greatest healer among all the great healers of the world.

Peret, the great French physician, said, "I treat the patient, but God alone can heal him." And I know a surgeon who, when he has completed an operation and is washing up, says, "Now, it's up to You." So Jesus Christ is still the supreme Master of human illness.

An important factor in the matter is this: Good emotions make us well; bad emotions make us sick. What are bad emotions? Anger, hate, resentment, fear. And what are good emotions? Faith, joy, happiness, love. Dr. John A. Schindler, in his book *How to Live 365 Days a Year*, says, "The Ochsner Clinic in New Orleans published a paper stating that 74 percent of 500 consecutive patients admitted to the department handling gastrointestinal diseases were

> *The House of God, ordinarily called a church, is actually a spiritual hospital to which people come with diseases: diseases in their bodies, in their minds, or in their souls. Here, the Great Physician touches them and makes them well.*

found to be suffering from emotionally induced illness." Imagine, all those people made ill because of bad emotions. That is not from the pulpit; that is from a clinic.

Dr. George Crile, who used to run a great clinic in Cleveland, years ago said there are three things that cause more human sickness than anything else: fear, anger, and guilt. They produce weariness and lack of vitality.

The House of God, ordinarily called a church, is actually a spiritual hospital to which people come with diseases: diseases in their bodies, in their minds, or in their souls. Here, the Great Physician touches them and makes them well. I really do believe this. "And the whole multitude sought to touch him: for there went virtue out of him, and healed them all" (Luke 6:19).

From disorder in our lives, and from bad emotions—as contrasted to good emotions—we develop illness. But illness can be cured by the mysterious healing power of faith. I don't pretend to understand this power. I only witness to the fact that it exists and performs wonders.

In some cases, healing doesn't come. That may be because proper conditions are not present in our lives. There comes a time for every man to die, but sometimes we can postpone this through the power of faith.

There is a wonderful book written by Gertrude McKelvey entitled *Finding God's Healing Power.* The author researched every center in this country where spiritual healing is practiced. She talked with men such as the Reverend Dr. Alfred Price, Bishop Austin Pardue, Dr. John Sutherland Bonnell, and other great men in this field.

She tells the story of a man named Wesley Hablett. I want to give it to you in her own words:

Wesley Hablett opened his eyes to see his surgeon standing quietly by his bed. He realized slowly that the doctor, whom we shall call Dr. Jones, had come to give him the final report on his operation. His thoughts now went back to his conversation with the surgeon just before entering the hospital.

"Dr. Jones, I can take it. I'm a grown man," he had said. "So promise me you will tell me the truth when you know it."

Five full days had passed since he had been wheeled back to his bed from surgery. For other patients about him in the small ward, this period meant healing and recovery. About his own case, he was not so sure, since his operation had been performed to remove a malignant tumor from his spine. Now, he would learn the truth.

Dr. Jones was reviewing the operation. He had found it possible to remove only part of the tumor, since cancer had spread, making it difficult to determine where the diseased cells stopped and the healthy cells began. Fifty-year-old Wesley Hablett, sensing the truth, went right to the point. "How long have I got, Dr. Jones?" he asked.

This outstanding neurological surgeon, a man of great faith, pulled the curtain around his patient's bed to ensure privacy, and sat down. This was not the first time he had been compelled to bring a hopeless report, yet each time it seemed more difficult.

He gave the answer quickly, "If you want to know how long I *think* you will live, then I would say about six months. But we both know that only God knows the answer."

A long silence followed, one of those times when, as so often happens in a doctor-patient relationship, a feeling of trust, compassion and gratitude akin to love possessed each. The surgeon broke the silence by asking: "Would you like me to pray with you?"

Wesley Hablett nodded. The surgeon's hand slipped into his pocket, came up with a small Testament from which he read quietly, then prayed. Another silence followed as these two men thought of their Savior and His redeeming love. They had not asked for healing, but for strength to carry out God's will for their lives.

Two weeks later, Dr. Jones was able to discharge his patient. He has remained in excellent physical condition for the past seven years, and his clinical tests, since the first six months after his operation, have all been negative. Wesley Hablett and his doctor had both felt a wonderful sense of the presence of God as they prayed together.

Do you feel His presence now? I do! In the depth of the stillness, which rests upon us when we truly pray, there is a mystic power by which man, who is both of the earth and of heaven, can be healed. Our lives were given by God. They can be taken by God. They can be healed by God. Let us touch Him.

EIGHT

*A*NTICIPATE A *G*OOD *O*UTCOME

All of us want to do the best we can with our lives. Life on earth is short at best, and if there are seventy-five or fifty or even twenty-five years behind you, and you are not satisfied that you have lived a creative life, you'd better get busy. Even though life is uncertain and insecure, it has tremendous possibilities, no matter how old you are or who you are.

Among the great principles that make life worthwhile is the anticipation of a good outcome. This is a subtle principle of creative living. We tend to draw back to ourselves that which we project in thought. If you send out a certain thought pattern continually, you are likely to draw back to yourself that same thought pattern. If you constantly project an image of bad outcomes, this is indeed a dangerous procedure, for it can, in effect, produce the kind of outcomes you project. If, on the contrary, you learn the great, vital, dynamic principle of anticipating good outcomes, then by a subtlety of the mind you set forces in motion that tend to produce good outcomes.

Sometime ago, I was talking with a man who is an industrial psychiatrist. He was telling me about a mutual friend who was having a hard time. Everyone recognized that this fellow had good training, an excellent education, above-average intelligence, and sterling character. The psychiatrist diagnosed his trouble in a picturesque way. He said the man had no knowledge of creative anticipation. I asked him to explain "creative anticipation."

The psychiatrist said that our friend was constantly anticipating bad results, both personally and in connection with his associates, and was thwarting his inherent potential, which was tremendous, by not using creative anticipation. He was, instead, using destructive anticipation, which brought to him destructive results.

Are you thinking in terms of destructive anticipation or creative anticipation? The Bible says much about this in many different ways. In Mark 11:24 it says, "Therefore I tell you, whatever you ask in prayer, believe that you have received it, and it will be yours" (RSV). That is a tremendous offer! And in Mark 11:23 it says, "Whoever . . . does not doubt in his heart, but believes that what he says will come to pass, it will be done for him" (RSV).

What is meant by "heart"? The heart is the instrument that pumps blood. But here, the Bible means to say that if, in your deep unconscious, you do not doubt what you pray for, you shall receive it. So anticipate good outcomes; do your best; leave it to God and believe it will come right!

I have preached this for years. If I had a tape recording of myself twenty-five years ago, it would say the same thing.

The reason is that it is basic truth, and basic truth never changes. You can think yourself into destructiveness, and many people do. They think themselves into ill health, into weakness, into failure, into old age. They don't really believe enough to think any other way. They anticipate the terrible way it's going to be, and then it actually becomes that way.

But it need not be like that. Remember the words of Jesus: "Whoever . . . does not doubt in his heart, but believes that what he says will come to pass, it will be done for him. Therefore I tell you, whatever you ask in prayer, believe that you have received it, and it will be yours."

There are many people who really believe in creative anticipation. They test it out. They put it into effect. A good example is this letter written to me by an advertising man:

> Some weeks ago, my agency was one of several invited to solicit for a substantial international advertising account. It is one of the largest companies in the world, employing over 300,000 people and doing an annual volume in excess of $5 billion.
>
> We were by far the smallest advertising agency invited to solicit for the account and, frankly, I was fearful that we would lose out because the other agencies had much more big-client experience.
>
> This past Tuesday was "Decision Day," and I knew the review meeting would be held in the company's offices at 10:45 A.M. I was haunted by the nagging fear that we were going to wind up as an also-ran, and I had

convinced myself with all of the reasons we wouldn't get this account.

I was awake most of the night before and was in a bad frame of mind on Tuesday morning. I sat in my office and wondered, "What can I do to convince these people that we are the right agency? Should I telephone and put in a final plea? Should I suggest a special fee arrangement that might offer them cash savings?"

Suddenly, I realized I hadn't used the most powerful convincer of all. I closed my office door, opened the Bible, and read and prayed. I also read two of your booklets, *Thought Conditioners* and *Spirit Lifters.* After a few moments, I closed my eyes and concentrated intently on all of the reasons we were ideally suited to handle this business. I saw very clearly that I should not do anything more, that it was in God's hands and He was working with me.

I opened my eyes, and, although the day had started out as a dull, dreary morning, suddenly the sun came out. I felt confident about the decision, which would be forthcoming any minute. An hour went by and I really had to keep a firm thought about the outcome.

Then the telephone rang. The caller said, "It was a tough meeting and a difficult decision. Frankly, we were leaning heavily in another direction, when someone pointed out that a smaller agency could give more personal and dedicated service, which is what our company badly needs. That was the turning point. In a few minutes, we made up our minds to go with your agency. I am happy to tell you that, instead of starting on July 1, you have our account effective today."

I know this decision was God-directed and God-inspired. It has helped me in my continuing growth to be more loving and understanding, and it has served as an excellent illustration to all of the members of my staff, who also realized that a power far greater than human power helped make this decision. It is the biggest account we have ever secured and has opened up an entirely new field for my firm.

This letter is a perfect illustration that your faith can be involved in everything you do all your life. Of course, good outcomes do not always come suddenly; sometimes a door is shut in your face. And often that is the best thing that can happen to you. For, as my dear mother used to tell me, "Norman, the door will slam in your face sometimes." (And don't think plenty of them haven't.) "This means that God is trying to guide you down the road to the open door that awaits you." So whatever things you ask and pray for, believe that you receive them and, if it is God's will, you will receive them.

To have good outcomes in your life, you also must be a good person. It is true that, sometimes, evil seems to prosper, and some people get away with things. But in the end, God collects His bills. The individual who has been a double-dealer gets it dealt to him. Good outcomes ultimately come to those people who justify good outcomes.

Therefore, we ought to be reminded that what we must develop in our country is a better, cleaner, more decent character in ourselves. A nation, as well as an individual, can go to pieces floundering on the lack of character. This is largely a responsibility of mothers. There is no one closer to a child than a mother. Of course, children also need their fathers—the family structure is important. But a mother is essential. And the kinds of mothers who made this country were gentle, feminine, beautiful, sweet women; but they were awfully tough, too! And they built character into their children. Our country will not continue to be great unless we make children, and all people, for that matter, amenable to the laws of righteousness and honor.

What do I know about children? I've raised three, with the help of my wife. And we're proud of them. Now I'm a grandfather, and this is quite a position.

One day, my daughter Liz deposited her nine-month-old son, Andrew, on my lap and asked, "Daddy, could you baby-sit for two hours with Andy?"

"What about your mother?" I asked.

"She's going shopping with me."

"Isn't there anyone else?" I hinted. "I'm busy; I'm dealing with important things."

She kissed me on the cheek and said, "There isn't anything more important than helping to direct the life of a child."

Well, since I was going to preach this same doctrine on Sunday, I had to get with it. Anyway, my grandson seemed comfortable. He was cooing and gurgling and smiling at me.

"We will be back in two hours," Liz announced. "I'll put him down to sleep now, and if he follows his usual pattern, he won't wake up. In case he does, here's a bottle; all you have to do is give it to him."

"How about diapers?" I wanted to know.

"I think we'll be safe on that," was her reply.

So, they hadn't been gone more than thirty minutes when I heard Andy crying. He screamed to high heaven! I went in and thought, *What's the matter with you? You're supposed to sleep for two hours.*

I picked him up and he stopped crying. I put him down;

You don't make great people by spraying them with perfume; you do it by love and discipline.

---

he yelled again. So I took him into the kitchen and took out the bottle. I warmed it up and gave it to him. This silenced him, but he gulped down the milk in no time.

I put him down after I'd given him the bottle. I thought that if his stomach was full, he would be satisfied. But he yelled again. I picked him up and he stopped; I put him down and he yelled. So I checked his diaper; he was dry. I sat down with him and said, "Look, Andy, let's have a talk. We must have an understanding. I don't know how your mother raises you, but I can tell you how your grandfather's going to do it. You can yell your head off until you get so tired that you fall down there and go to sleep. I'm not going to pick you up anymore. So get with it."

What do you think happened? The little fellow, not yet a year old, gave me a great big laugh. He didn't cry again. It was as if he understood and said to himself, "I can't fool with this guy, so I'd better obey orders and be good."

Today, I know we have many soft people who don't think that is the way to do things. But you don't make great people by spraying them with perfume; you do it by love and discipline. Now, I wouldn't have strongly disciplined my grandson at that age. He's lovable; he really gets around your heartstrings. But I was firm because I love him.

You know, there is nothing in God's world like this mother-child relationship. Only God could have thought of it. It is so subtle, so profound. A mother who can have rapport with a young child is a genius, and only God can make her so.

I was once driving behind a school bus from Carmel to Pawling, New York, which is an exercise in patience because you have to stop when it does. But I was glad I followed this one. We were stopped beside a lake, and on the other side were some scattered houses. A boy about nine years old got off the bus. He tossed his pile of books to the side as he picked up a flat rock and skipped it across the lake. It was the most beautiful sight, the rock bouncing from wavelet to wavelet. I wanted to grab a rock myself to see if I could go him one better.

Then the boy started walking toward the house, carrying his books. His mother was home waiting for him, which is indeed significant. She waved to him and came bouncing down the walk. She was a beautiful woman and she was smart, too, for she didn't kiss him. There's a time when men like to be kissed, but it isn't at nine years of age. So what did she do? She put up her hands like a prizefighter and she socked him a couple of times in the chest. Then they turned around and went up the walk together. It was the boy who put his arm around his mother's waist. And she, being taller, put her arm around his shoulder. They walked into the house.

Entranced by it all—the bus was almost out of sight—I thought, *What a mother!* And when that boy is an old man, and the years have mounted up, and death is knocking at his door, it wouldn't surprise me if the last name he mentions is the name *Mother*. That kind of a mother builds the anticipation of good outcomes into children. She makes them good so that they're worthy of good outcomes. And people like that make our nation good, and solid, and right. We must keep it that way!

Let us all dedicate ourselves to building good outcomes. Practice the great principle of creative, spiritual anticipation in your life, and it will be full of good outcomes!

NINE
FAITH CAN LIFT YOU UP

Looking over an audience, I often wonder about all the sorrows, the problems, the hopes, the dreams, the frustrations that are represented. How many human heartaches are present?

Once in Japan, I had a nice visit with a Shinto priest who told me he and his coreligionists considered that there are fifteen basic human problems. When I asked him to name them, he replied, "You name them!" Which is to say that my list and his list would be equally valid. Well, whether there are fifteen or fifty, the Gospel of Jesus Christ is the right place to look to for the right answer to any problem.

One of the most remarkable statements ever made, a statement that is almost incredible, and one that offers enormous hope, is found in Matthew 17:20: "If ye have faith as a grain of mustard seed, ye shall say unto this mountain, Remove hence to yonder place; and it shall remove; and nothing shall be impossible unto you." Another version says, "If you have faith as big as a mustard seed, you can say to this hill, 'Go from here to there!' and it will go. You could do anything!" (TEV).

> *Jesus Christ teaches that many of the greatest things in this world are done not by something big but by something small. But that something small must be packed full of power and reality.*

These are words from the most reliable mind that ever appeared on this earth. It is interesting that the great philosophers of the past who are studied today have nothing like the enormous influence on people that Jesus has. All that remains from these scholars is a body of writing; what remains from Him is a Person, a Person with the Truth. Since this passage comes from Jesus, we can believe it. And whatever your difficulty may be, you can gain a victory over it by applying the truth of this passage.

The first thing it tells us is that all it takes is to have faith as a grain of mustard seed. That means not much faith, only a little—yes, just a speck. It isn't necessary to recite all the creeds and doctrines of the church. All you have to have is a little bit of faith, but this must be real. Jesus Christ teaches that many of the greatest things in this world are done not by something big but by something small. But that something small must be packed full of power and reality.

One time, in a newspaper that reported interesting phenomena, I read about a professor who performed a demonstration for some purpose or other. His equipment consisted of a board, a big nail, a bottle, and a small fleck of Carborundum. He took the bottle in his right hand—it was a big, thick, heavy bottle, one of the thickest, heaviest bottles you could get—and he used it as a hammer. With a series of powerful strokes of the bottle, he drove the nail into the board. This didn't fragmentize the bottle. Then the professor took the tiny fleck of Carborundum, which is one of the hardest of the solids, and dropped it into the glass bottle. The bottle was instantly shattered into many pieces. It wasn't size or quantity that did it; it was essence.

So it is with the problems and difficulties of this life. Suppose you bring to bear against your difficulties all the force and power that you can, all the struggling that you can, all the resisting of which you are capable, but it isn't effective. Then take a mustard-seed pinch of faith and drop it with confidence into the problem. The problem shatters, breaks apart; it reveals to you all the elements of the problem, and you put it together for a solution.

No wonder that Jesus Christ, the divine Son of God, the Redeemer, has lived all these years as the *one* great figure who has compelling influence over the human race, because He deals with the essence of things. The essence of the matter, in the beginning of our text, is that the faith referred to isn't genial, Pollyannaish kind of faith; it is faith in-depth. This doesn't come easily. But when you have it, then you have the faith that moves mountains, that can accomplish anything. It is an extraordinary power.

Jesus also tells us, in the same statement, that faith eliminates one of the most overwhelming factors in human experience: the impossible. *It's impossible,* one thinks, *that I could better this situation* or *that I could solve this problem* or *that I could overcome this difficulty* or *that I could conquer this sorrow. It's impossible!* But, when you have this mustard-seed pinch of faith, you no longer see it as impossible.

This doesn't mean that you will get everything you want. That would not be desirable or wise. It does mean that, hereafter, it is no longer impossible that a great life shall be yours. This is what the Bible proclaims.

Let me give you two other quotes. Mark 9:23: "If thou canst believe. . . ." The hardest thing in the world, maybe, is to believe. It is a struggle, it doesn't come easily; but when you learn to believe, ". . . all things are possible to him that believeth." Now, that is rather difficult. *All* things are possible if you can believe. Again, there is the statement in Luke 18:27: "The things which are impossible with men are possible with God."

Take the social situation in which we live today. Some believe that the only way to correct social injustice is through sociological procedures and legislative action. I personally believe in both sociological and legislative action. But this is not the main thing, or the most important. What would change the social situation in this country and the world today, and change it within a short period of time, would be a great turning of the people to belief in God. For that which is impossible to man is possible with God. That is why we should support every movement, every design, to bring the power not of man but of God into social action.

"Well," you may say, "it sounds good. But you don't know what a tough problem *I* have. You don't know the impossibilities *I* face." Yes, I do! I haven't been a pastor all these years without knowing what people face. I have a deep and profound compassion for human beings. All of us are poor souls struggling in this world of difficulty. I know how hard your problems are, all right. But, however appalling our problems are, we are to have faith in God; for He is equal to them all.

Let me share with you a letter. It is from a nineteen-year-old girl. I will not tell you who she is, for obvious reasons, or even in what part of the country she lives. And I have changed the name of the boy in the letter, since this is highly confidential. Sadly, I receive more and more letters like this all the time. Here is this one:

Dear Dr. Peale,

If anyone had told me even a week ago that I would be writing this, I would probably have laughed out loud. I'm 19 years old and have for quite some time called myself an atheist. But, last week, I went to a doctor. He told me I am pregnant. I am not married.

This news has, needless to say, changed my life completely. Now I realize how terribly wrong I was in bringing a new life into this world under such wrong circumstances. Also, I'm afraid that Jack's feelings have changed toward me. I'm sure at one time he loved me, but I am so afraid that he doesn't care anymore. I don't know what I will do if he doesn't care anymore.

But what frightens me even more than all this is that for the past two years I have been taking drugs. I was just after a few kicks, but now I may have ruined another life. God help me. I know I was wrong. I also know I can't retrace my steps and change things. But at least I now realize my mistakes and I'm trying to rectify them.

Night before last, I was sitting in the living room, sulking. I was convinced the whole world was against me, that my life was ruined and that I had no future. My roommate came in with some of your sermon pamphlets. She suggested that I read a couple of them, so, to pacify her, I did. I can't believe how different I am because of those pamphlets. They made me realize how much I need Someone stronger than me. The situation seems so impossible. Is there any hope?

At nineteen one should be happy. For a girl of nineteen, the world should be filled with promise. This terrible thing that we call sin has soured the mixture. We read in certain publications about getting high on drugs and the new morality, how fulfilling it is. The real truth comes out when you come up against a story like this one. And believe me, the woods—or the streets—are full of it.

Is there any hope for this girl? I wrote to her and told her what I now tell you and myself: that if she will commit herself completely, and I do mean completely, to Jesus Christ and develop in-depth faith, she can reconstruct her life and nothing need be hopeless; that she can eliminate the impossibilities from her life. As a reborn and remade child of God, she can become a beautiful mother and raise a marvelous child. Why? Because God loves her even though she has done a terribly wrong thing.

So you name your impossible problem and take a great big red pencil and write, "I have faith in Christ and I thereby strike a line through that word *impossible.*" Jesus deals in the truth about life and people. So, through faith in Him, the impossibility factor can be removed.

The mustard-seed passage is a tremendous text. It is just full of values. First, there is the power of just a little faith—which has to be real. Second, it eliminates impossibility. Third, it eliminates the mountains.

In these passages, the Bible speaks figuratively about mountains. If you walked up a hill and tried to tell it to get out of your way, the hill would say, "The only way you can get me out of the way is to bring a power shovel and bulldozer. That will get me out of the way." What is meant in the Bible by a mountain is that accumulation of stuff in your life that obstructs you: mistakes, weaknesses, sins, frustrations, mixed-up thinking. All this gets in your way and blocks your path.

And how are you going to get rid of it? Walk up to it with faith! If you have faith even as a grain of mustard seed, you should say to this mountain, "Be thou removed" and believe. There is another passage, in Matthew 21:21, that says if you have faith you can say to the mountain,

> *The person who has the mustard seed of profound*
> *faith never accepts defeat, because he knows he*
> *can scatter defeat to the winds.*

"Be thou removed, and be thou cast into the sea" and it shall be done. ". . . cast into the sea. . . ." That means out of sight, swallowed up, rid of completely.

So what is standing between you and a great life, a beautiful life, a godly life, a life worthwhile? It may be your ability to believe, your acceptance of defeat. Never accept defeat. The person who has the mustard seed of profound faith never accepts defeat, because he knows he can scatter defeat to the winds.

Once, when I was on a speaking trip, I checked in at a certain hotel. It seemed like a nice hotel and, when I went to my room, I was sure it was a nice hotel. Not only was the room attractive but on the dresser was a beautiful arrangement of flowers and on the table an enormous basket of fruit. I thought, *I wonder how much all this is going to cost me?* Then I examined the slip the bellboy had handed me. And what do you know? It said, "Complimentary," which completely changed my attitude toward the whole matter! So, without delay, I went downstairs to call on the manager, who was responsible for all these benefits. "I want to thank you for the fruit and the flowers and the complimentary room," I said. "You didn't need to do all that."

"I wanted to," he replied. "I wanted to do it because of what you have done for me."

"Because of what I have done for you? What in the world did I ever do for you?"

"Oh," he said, "a nurse and you saved my life."

Well, this was interesting and humbling, and I pressed him to tell me the story. He explained: "Some years ago, I had a stroke, which was a great blow to me. It rendered my left side paralyzed, interfered with the left side of my mouth, and disturbed my speech. I lay in bed and thought, *I am just a remnant of a man. I don't amount to anything anymore. I have had it. I am all through.*

"But the doctors took good care of me and I was slowly recovering. One day, our family doctor came to see me and said, 'You are much better. Your reactions are much improved. If you will, you can be a well man.'"

He was a wise doctor, for equally as important as medicine is your will to get well. That doctor knew that this man would need a mighty will because he had a great big mountain in front of him. So he told him, "If you make up your mind to do it, you can get out of bed and you can walk."

"But my arm," said the man, "it's limp."

The doctor assured him, "The arm will recover. And your speech is already much improved."

Now the man had a fine nurse. I have great respect for the profession of nursing. Some of the greatest people I have ever met have been nurses—loving, understanding, giving themselves completely to human beings. This nurse brought the man one of my books and he read it and he thought, *This is great, but it doesn't apply to a man in my condition.* He read in that book, he told me, the passage I have quoted. "If ye have faith as a grain of mustard seed . . . nothing shall be impossible unto you." He thought, *I believe that.* But he didn't really; he only thought he believed; he didn't really believe it would work in his case.

So after a few days, the nurse came and lowered the side of the bed. She pulled back the covers and said, "Get out of bed. Are you a man or are you a worm? Put your hand in mine, think of the Lord Jesus Christ, and get out of bed."

Now, medically, she knew what she was doing, and psychologically and spiritually she also knew. He put his foot down gingerly.

"I followed her," he told me, "in a staggering fashion to the door of my room. There, she let go of my hand, and she said, 'Now go on your own. But remember, Jesus Christ will hold you up.' I looked at her and I knew she believed it, and suddenly I did, too." He then got up from behind his desk and walked around, and all I could see was a slight limp of the left leg. He concluded, "I am manager of this big, fine hotel and have all these opportunities, because I learned to believe." The mountain had melted out of his way.

Faith can indeed lift you up—and hold you up!

TEN

HOW TO RELAX

A great many people today are tense and nervous. This is a predominant characteristic of our times. But really, people do not need to be so tense. The tension of modern living has invaded the quiet sanctuary of the soul and of the central nervous system as well. This is an era of crises. When I think back to when I was a boy, it seems a peaceful period compared with this day. No wonder the incidence of nervous diseases has grown so rapidly. It is an age that is afflicted with tension.

This problem is adversely and profoundly affecting the happiness and well-being of people. One cannot believe that the good Lord wants His children to be thus afflicted. Surely He hopes that in our hearts and minds we will find and enjoy the blessings of peace and serenity.

How, then, can we stop being tense? Well, let me tell you about a man who kept calling me long distance about once a week, telling me that he was so tense he could almost "jump out of my skin"—as he put it. He called hoping I might say something peaceful and soothing that would quiet him. Of course I was sympathetic and tried to do my best for him. But he kept calling more and more often. I soon

> *One of the greatest dangers of human nature is*
>
> *to become a leaner, to transfer your own*
>
> *sense of responsibility to someone else.*

realized that he was leaning on me; I had become a kind of father to him, just because I was trying to help him.

One of the greatest dangers of human nature is to become a leaner, to transfer your own sense of responsibility to someone else. It is a human weakness that can get badly out of hand. Anyway, this man did not know what a slender reed he was leaning on.

"Say something to me that will help me stop being tense," he kept repeating with a kind of desperation. "The only way I get any relief is to pick up the telephone and call you," he explained miserably.

One night when he called—and he called at all hours—I said to him, "Instead of dialing me, why don't you dial a Book that you have in your possession? It will save you money and will do you more good." My suggestion mystified him, so I explained that I would give him several passages of Scripture designed to help him escape tension. "Just dial the Book and say those Scripture passages to yourself," I suggested.

I convinced him that this was a good idea, and he agreed to try it. One of the passages I gave him was Psalm 46:10:

"Be still, and know that I am God." He told me later that this one verse pulled him out of his difficulty.

"What I discovered," he said, "is that you must have inner stillness to overcome tension. And the way you get inner stillness is to stop your agitation just long enough to realize that God is God, that you are in His hands, that He watches over you and guides you, and that you can depend upon Him. When you are agitated, you forget Him. In fact, you cannot think of anything constructive. But when you become quiet, you begin to understand, you think things out rationally and sensibly, and your tension lessens."

What a tremendous truth! Just be quiet, get calm, and remember, He is God. You will realize that you need not be upset or disturbed; He is with you and can do anything for you. That is the meaning of this Scripture. So get your mind on God: off your troubles, off your hates, off your conflicts. Practice this wonderful tension-reducing technique. "Be still, and know that I am God."

If there is any one quality we must get into our systems, it is stillness. Pascal, seventeenth-century philosopher, said, "One of the ways in which man brings the most trouble upon himself is by his inability to be still." You have to learn to have inner stillness. That does not mean you are not to be active, but you cannot be forever active unless you are also still. Edwin Markham, the poet, said, "At the heart of the cyclone tearing the sky is a place of central calm." That is to say, the cyclone derives its power from a calm center. So does a person. No one can have driving force and energy unless he is also a master of stillness.

A wise bit of advice: "Be still, and know that I am God." Get spiritual stillness in your body, in your mind, and in your soul. This is the trinity that makes up the individual.

The body is the greatest instrument ever made; it is given to you to make your life rich and full; it is given to you to use. As far as we know, you will never have this kind of body again; it is the only one you are ever going to have. The next body you get will be a spiritual one, and the more spiritual you make this body you now occupy, the more natural will be the shift to the spiritual one. Indeed, your body is so sacred that it is often referred to as the temple of the soul.

But it is a complicated instrument. The ability to raise your arm—or to open and shut your eyes, or eat, or speak—is something no earthly inventor knows how to reproduce. In overcoming tension, you can start by practicing quietness and stillness in your physical body.

Note the various nervous movements of the hands—drumming the fingers, stroking the cheek, nail biting—all evidences of muscle tension in the body.

Years ago, I became convinced that muscle tension had so much to do with mental tension that I decided to practice bodily stillness techniques and found them effective. In the course of my study, I went to a Hindu swami's relaxation demonstration. That man sat for one solid hour without twitching a muscle. In trying the same procedure, I could hardly stand it. I could even hear myself swallow.

Later, I developed more ability to reduce muscle tension. The secret is to relax and think of every part of your body as quiet and still—that God is giving His peace to your muscles and nerves. That is a great art to master.

It is even possible to practice stillness of the body in the midst of tumult. One way to do this is to lie down on some fairly flat surface, such as the floor, where you can keep the backbone straight and the organs in proper balance. Start with your feet and say, "The stillness of God is in my toes, my feet . . ." and come up through every part of your body saying, "The stillness of God is in my heart, my lungs, my stomach, my fingers, my arms; the muscles of my neck, the muscles of my face, the lids of my eyes. . . ." It is as if to say, "Be still, O physical organs, and know that I am God."

A woman told me she practices physical relaxation on the basis of the body being the temple of the soul. As part of this process, she lets her tongue rest for ten minutes on the floor of her mouth. She claims, and I think she is right, that the tongue is related to the muscles of the throat and face and that these, in turn, are related to the general attitude of the body. You may discover some other technique, but however you do it, I strongly recommend that you consciously relax and conceive of the hand of Jesus as touching every part of your body.

How would you feel if you met Jesus when you were tense, and He put His hand on your heart? Wouldn't that be wonderful in its quieting effect? Or if you had pain—to feel His hand where your pain was. Why not? He says He is with us always. He comes to you when you seek Him. He touches your body and gives you stillness.

Then there is the necessity of cultivating stillness in the mind. If you could flush out of your mind all the sins you have ever committed, wouldn't you have stillness? Suppose you could mentally lose any sense of injustice that agitates you—wouldn't you have inner stillness?

The cause of tension is often disturbance due to some sin you have committed that was never forgiven. Or, it may be you are struggling with some temptation or compromise that keeps you tense. If you have a sense of injustice and resentment, or ill will, you can have no stillness. But as the Bible tells us, we can be washed clean and become whiter than snow (Psalm 51:7).

I remember a man who had a virulent hatred for a former employer. Everything the employer had done was wrong. Only vaguely would he admit that anything he himself had done was wrong. That, of course, was inconceivable. This poor fellow was seething. The look on his face, when he talked of the man, made one aware of his intensity of feeling. And he kept telling the bitter story over and over.

Finally, he developed many symptoms of hypertension until a minister took him into a church and made him kneel at the altar. He said to him, "Your trouble is because of the hatred in your system. You are filled with all manner of resentment, and I want you to stay here at the altar until it is all washed out. Unless you do so, your tension will destroy you."

The cleansing took place; the man gained quietness, peace, and composure. His tension was gone.

Developing mental stillness is a great art. The ability to control your mind in the midst of tense circumstances, to send your mind into some area of peace and quietness, is hard to come by. Yet, it is remarkable what you can do with your mind in developing quietness and composure. When you are in a tense situation, by means of your thoughts you can go away from where you are, however hectic, into a place of quietness and peace.

The famous former Brooklyn Dodger pitcher, and my good friend, Carl Erskine, told me how he kept calm and confident in the midst of the confusion and pressure of a ball game.

"I have a little trick," he said. "When I get in a tight spot, I pick up the ball and walk around the pitcher's mound, thinking of a creek in Indiana where I fish. I remember how cool and peaceful it is on a beautiful morning, when I throw a line into the still water. Mentally, I go fishing."

Imagine crowds of fans, sitting wondering what ball Erskine was going to pitch, while he went fishing in Indiana! You can go away in your mind to any place you like—and you can go without buying a plane ticket. You might go up into the North Country, where the aroma of pine and hemlock is in the air. You can go down by the sea, watching the water lap gently on the sand. With your mind, in the turning of a thought, you can be with God, sharing His everlasting peace. Bring this quietness of God into any situation and note the results.

There is a deeper experience of quietness for human nature than even those of the body or mind. It is when, at long last, the soul stands in the presence of God; when the soul yields itself to God; when you take everything in your life and put it into the hands of God, believing that if you do your best, you can safely leave it with Him. Then your tension passes away—like the old Indian's interpretation of the Twenty-third Psalm. He said the phrase "thou anointest my head with oil" (verse 5) means, "He puts His hand on my head and all the tired goes 'way." The oil, symbol of the everlasting peace of God, is given to people who have become still in their bodies, minds, and souls. Then they are no longer in a dither of nervous tension as to what life is going to do for them, or to them. They do the best they can and leave the rest to God. God does the best He can, and that is enough.

Life can be wonderful, victorious, overwhelming, if you will just get this stillness of God into your body, mind, and soul. Do the best you can; do good, be good. Then put it all into His hands and trust Him. Don't be excited; don't be nervous; don't be tense. Just be still. Remember that He is God, and He will give the peace and power of God to you.

Scriptures for Relaxing Tension

Peace, be still. *(Mark 4:39)*

Peace I leave with you, my peace I give unto you. *(John 14:27)*

And the peace of God, which passeth all understanding, shall keep your hearts and minds through Christ Jesus.

(Philippians 4:7)

Come unto me, all ye that labour and are heavy laden, and I will give you rest.

(Matthew 11:28)

Be still, and know that I am God.

(Psalm 46:10)

ELEVEN
DRAW UPON THE HIGHER POWER

Do you ever feel inadequate in the presence of the problems of human existence? Do you ever feel the need for more power within yourself? I am sure it is safe to say that everyone does at one time or another. Well, I want to remind you that God, through faith in Jesus Christ, builds power into people, so that they become equal to whatever life may bring.

I was talking with a man who told me of an experience he had following a game of golf. It was one of the great spiritual incidents of his life. He and two other men were concerned about a friend of theirs who was having a great deal of trouble. "So," he said, "we three fellows ganged up on George and took him out to the golf course with us to get his mind off himself."

They had a pleasant game. Afterward, as they were sitting in the locker room in the clubhouse, George spoke up and said, "I want to thank you fellows. I know what you are up to, getting me out here today to play golf. This was your way of helping me. I want you to know I am touched by it.

You certainly are good friends. For the three hours we were on the course, I did sort of forget my troubles for a time. But, whether I can handle the problems I am faced with, I don't know. Life has thrown the whole book at me. I just don't know what to do."

At this point, one of the other men rose, ready to leave. He dropped his hand on George's shoulder and said, "Look, George, I haven't known you too long, but I think I know how you feel. A few years ago, so many things were going wrong for me that I thought no one ever had such troubles. It just seemed that I couldn't handle them at all. I was about to give up. As a matter of fact, I had what you might call the makings of a nervous breakdown. But then I met a man who really had something. This man had had a spiritual experience in-depth, and his whole being was full of power. One day he said to me, 'The only way you will ever solve your problems is to draw upon the higher power.' So look, friend, you do the same. Draw upon the higher power."

The man telling about this said that the phrase struck him, for he, too, had troubles he had not said anything about—and even the good game of golf hadn't dissipated them. He went home thinking about that statement, "Draw upon the higher power." Of course, he knew the reference was to God. *How,* he thought, *can I draw on that power? I know it is of God, but I haven't got it.* Then it occurred to him that God didn't just create us and set us down here by ourselves, isolated: He maintains a contact and He keeps it

> *God didn't just create us and set us down here by ourselves, isolated: He maintains a contact and He keeps it open, always. And through this contact, power—divine power—can flow into us.*

open, always. And through this contact, power—divine power—can flow into us.

"Well," the man continued, "as I was thinking about this one day, I had the most releasing experience. All of a sudden, it seemed I was infused with power from on high. I was able to cast out all my negativisms, all my fears, all my hates, all my weaknesses, all my tension, and my nervousness. I got power over myself right then and there. I tell you, it's a fact: Any human being who really makes the effort, who isn't content just to wallow forever in his weaknesses, but who makes the effort, can draw upon this higher power!"

He then gave me a text. He said it was his personal, private text, but actually it isn't so personal and private, for he shares it with everyone, as he shared it with me. I, too, take it as my text—and I give it to you.

It is Luke 18:27: "The things which are impossible with men are possible with God." It means you do not need to have any impossibles at all. You can draw upon the power from God that moves the impossibles into the area of the possibles. Draw upon that higher power.

Don't take this for granted. Take it as though you had never heard anything like it before. *You do not need to be defeated.* You can draw upon the higher power. *Really* pull it down into yourself, into your life, and spread it out everywhere. This is a tremendous thing! Take it! Listen to it! Grab it!

But you may be wondering how in the world to do it. *How* do you draw on that higher power? Well, you *live* with God. You live with Him every day. You live with Christ. You talk to Him. You walk with Him. You pray to Him. You think about Him. You don't do anything, however seemingly small or insignificant, that you don't bring Him into it. Some people never think of God except in connection with church or some religious exercise. Other people live with Him every minute of the day. The more you do this, the more the power flow increases.

I have a friend in Toronto, for example, a businessman and a good one—top-notch in his line. He prays about everything. He talks with God as he walks down the street. And he prays that every day the Lord will lead him to someone he can help.

He told me he was walking along a Toronto street one day when it occurred to him to go into a certain men's clothing shop. This shop was operated by a young couple, friends of his. He noticed, as he came close to the window, that the place was unpainted, looked drab, and was dimly lighted inside. He knew these young friends carried high-quality merchandise, but the place repelled him instead of attracting him. He went in. There were no customers in the store. The wife was attending to something behind the counter toward the back. The husband was upstairs in the office. My friend asked, "Mary, how are things going? I just felt I should come in and see you."

"Oh," she replied, "things are bad. We may have to fold. I don't know if we can hang on to this business."

"What is the trouble?"

"Come upstairs and see John," she said. "He's up there fussing over bills. There are no customers here, so it doesn't make any difference if I go up with you."

She took him up to the office, which was on a balcony. And there was John. He had a great stack of bills he was getting ready to send out. "I don't know what I am going to do," he said. "We can't get anyone to pay us promptly, and our business has fallen off. We put in a big inventory. Our suppliers are pressing us. What are we going to do?"

"Well," my friend said to him, "there's a paint store down the street. One thing you can do is to go down and get a can of paint and a brush and, after you close up at night, just go around and paint all the woodwork an attractive color. It will brighten the place up. And for goodness' sake, get yourself some new light fixtures. Flood the place with light. Anyone who knows how to merchandise anything knows you have to have color; you have to have light; you have to display the goods well. So why don't you get busy doing it?"

"Oh, that wouldn't do any good," the young man answered in a discouraged tone.

"Now, about those bills. Do you know the people you sold these goods to?"

"We know a few of them."

"Can you call them by name?"

"No," said John, "we can call hardly any of them by name."

"Well, this one here: William Smith. How many children has he got?"

"I haven't the slightest idea," replied John.

"Or this Mr. Jones. How's his wife, do you know?"

"Why, I don't even know whether he is married. What's all this got to do with it?"

"What you've got to do," my friend told him, "is to bring God into this business. You've got to get so much God in the heart that you begin to love these people. Don't just be interested in selling them shirts and ties but be interested in them as persons. Maybe they need much more than a shirt or a tie. Maybe they need courage and hope and faith. Why don't you give that to them? What are you going to do right now? Send those bills out?"

"Yes," said the young storekeeper, "we've got to. We've got to get six hundred dollars, and we've got to get it fast. We are that near failing."

"All right," said the older man. "Mary, you come over here. And John, you come over here." He put his hand on the stack of bills and got them to put their hands on top of his. He prayed aloud, "Dear Lord, here are Mary and John. They are running this store, and they really don't know how to do it. They need You as a partner. Help them, won't You?

"Now, they are going to send these bills out to all these people, and we ask You to bless all who receive them. Bless Mr. Jones's wife, if he has one. Bless Mr. Smith's children, if he has any. Be with those among these people who are sick. Send the power of faith down through these bills. And, dear Lord, make us love these people."

Did you ever hear of running a business that way? Well, this was the practical result: One week later, the couple had nine hundred dollars in the till, three hundred dollars more than they desperately needed. And many customers who couldn't pay wrote notes about how kind and patient the owners had been. John and Mary hadn't expressed kindness in any tangible way. They had sent it mentally through the power of God.

Soon, more people began to come to the shop, which, meanwhile, the owners had brightened up. They drew upon the higher power. And, the great thing about it wasn't that their business increased; it was what happened to them personally. They became two of the most vital members of one of the great churches in Toronto.

So make a fresh evaluation of the kind of life you live. How deeply involved is God in your everyday life? Whatever your problem, take God into it. Draw upon the higher power.

There are also the deep, hard experiences in life: great pain, great sorrow, the anguish of bereavement, the tension and anxiety that come when a loved one is seriously ill. Everyone has to face such things at one time or another, in one way or another. There will come a time when you think you just haven't got the strength to meet the situation you face. But you have, really, for Almighty God has put a wonderful power into human beings. He is an astonishing Creator. I am not thinking only of the physical mechanism He has made, the body, but of the resiliency of spirit He put into us.

Greater than anything else, He has given us the capacity to have faith—to let something go and let Him take it over. This is really one of the greatest secrets of human existence: Do all you can about a thing and, having done all, turn it over to God. When there is nothing more you can do about a situation, what more can you do? It is then that you turn it over to God, put it into His hands, leave it with Him; rest it with Him confidently, expectantly, prayerfully, and with faith. He may not give you the answer you want, but He will give you the answer you should have. He will always do right by you. Have the faith to trust Him. Put your problem into His hands and the power will come through.

Years ago, while flying low over Chicago, I looked down and saw the old Edgewater Beach Hotel, where I have made many speeches. In its time, it was a great hotel. Well, I remember speaking in the ballroom of the Edgewater Beach Hotel at a luncheon meeting of a big national convention. The place was packed, and at the end of the room a line of waitresses stood listening. They were all dressed in black, with white collars and cuffs, a very attractive, young group.

When the meeting was over, I had to get away in a hurry because of another commitment. As I was walking across the ballroom entrance, which had a floor of huge squares of marble, I heard someone running behind me, obviously a woman, her heels striking on the stone floor. Turning around, I saw one of the waitresses. She rushed up to me, grabbed my arms, and said, "Oh, Dr. Peale, I really love you!"

I looked at her, and she had such a sweet, happy face that I said, "You know something? I love you, too." Then I said, "But, please enlighten me: Why do we love each other?"

By this time, four or five other waitresses had gathered around. She answered, "Oh, it is because of an idea I got out of one of your printed sermons. I have a little boy. He is a sweetheart, and I love him. His father is gone. I have only the boy left. Well, he became ill. He was so sick that the doctor called me in one day and said, 'Mary, I've got to tell you. I don't think this boy can live. You must strengthen yourself. You may lose your boy. I'll do all I can, but I have to give it to you straight.'

"And I said, 'Oh, doctor, I *can't* lose him! I mustn't lose him! He's all I have! He's all I live for!' " And she told how she went and told her next-door neighbor about it. This neighbor got out one of our sermons. You never know about a piece of printed material, where it may fill a need. The neighbor said, "You read this."

Well, in that sermon was the advice that when a loved one is ill, and you've done all you can, then the thing is to pray, "Lord, You gave me this loved one. I give him back to You. I put him in Your hands. No harm can come to him because Your heart is so loving and Your arms are so strong.

So I just put him back in Your hands. I give him to You. I wish You would let me keep him, but if You can't, I'll understand."

The young woman continued, "I had never read anything like that. It astonished me. But somehow it seemed the right thing to do. So I prayed and said, 'Lord, here he is. I give him to You. I put him in Your hands. You take him. If you can just let me have him back, I'll thank You so much. But if You can't, I'll know You will give me the power to take it.' "

At this point, I noticed there were tears in the eyes of everyone listening, including myself. I asked, "What happened finally?"

"Thank God," she said, "he did get well! God did give him back to me. But you know, I felt such wonderful power and peace. I've dedicated my boy to being a good Christian. I am going to love him into it."

> *The average individual does not live up to*
> *his greatest possibilities more than a few times*
> *in his whole life. We are infinitely greater*
> *than we ordinarily act.*

I looked at her and said, "You are one of the greatest mothers I've ever met. You have found the answer for you and your child." The other waitresses nodded their heads.

That young woman drew upon the higher power. What is impossible with men becomes possible with God. And this higher power is available to each of us. The average individual does not live up to his greatest possibilities more than a few times in his whole life. We are infinitely greater than we ordinarily act. I wish I could make you see what you really can be through the power of God in Jesus Christ. Put yourself, and everything you love and hope for, in God's hands. Draw upon the higher power.

TWELVE

PRAYER CAN CHANGE YOUR LIFE

There is something that, when you find it, will make your life absolutely wonderful. It is all tied up with Someone you can't see but who is real just the same. And when this Someone gets through to you and me, our lives are changed. I haven't the slightest doubt about this, for many times I have seen people who were defeated, mixed-up, and sinful turn to God, receive Him, and be wonderfully changed. Prayer is fundamental in this life-changing experience, and I strongly recommend that you learn the art of prayer and put it to work in your life.

I once sat in the ballroom of a hotel in Toronto, Ontario, with a gathering of Canadian advertising and sales people. I was the speaker for this occasion, and the audience seemed very sophisticated. I remarked to the man sitting on my right, with whom I had just become acquainted, that I felt power in the room and thought it must be from the quality of these people.

"Oh," he said, "don't be so sure the power is from these people. I've been praying for this meeting."

This was rather startling, because I hadn't expected to encounter such spiritual ardor. I sometimes forget that there is an immense spiritual stirring in people's hearts.

The man then said to me, "I found two things that have made everything in life different for me. The first—and the greatest single experience I have ever had—was finding Jesus Christ and committing my life to Him. The second was that I learned to pray. These two things," he declared, "revolutionized my life." He added, "What a pity so many human beings never find Christ and never learn to pray! They miss the greatest values in this life."

This is what Jesus has been saying to us through the years, and really astute people make this discovery. Prayer can change your life. It has been my privilege to be associated with many people who have had this experience in one way or another.

When I say this of prayer, I do not mean mere mumbling of words. I do not mean formal affirmations, either, although formal prayers sometimes help, and some formal prayers are touched with the glory of God. What I mean is a deep, fundamental, powerful relationship with God, whereby your whole mind and heart become changed and you receive power from the Source. I have seen such prayer change the lives of so many.

Some people think you come to such a change in only one way. Nothing could be more false. Springtime comes in more ways than one. If it were standardized, if you saw the same thing wherever you looked, spring would not have the glory it has.

After the meeting in Toronto, I drove to Buffalo, New York, through the fruit orchards of Ontario. I'd never before been through that region in the springtime. And it was wonderful. The orchards were ablaze with white and pink. The blossoms stretched as far as you could see, from the shores of Lake Erie back inland. The whole atmosphere was full of a subtle fragrance. The air was clear and fresh and cold.

Springtime in some areas is soft and balmy. It is not the same everywhere. And Christ comes like springtime in different ways to different hearts. Sometimes He comes through feelings, sometimes through the mind; sometimes He comes through theology, sometimes through scientific reasoning; sometimes He comes through poetry. Sometimes He comes in simple ways, sometimes in complicated ways. As the human heart and mind are conditioned, so does He come. But however He comes, associated with Him is the life of prayer.

Thinking along these lines, my mind goes back over many experiences. I remember one night when I spoke in a suburban church in a midwestern city. A man came up to me and asked if he could drive me back to my hotel. This man's manner was so appealing that I let my other transportation go and went with him. He was a hail-fellow-well-met kind of person, and I liked him right off. He led me down the street to the most battered automobile I think I've ever seen. "How do you like that for a car?" he asked.

"Oh," I said, "that sure is some car." (It may have been, about twenty years before!)

"Well," he said, "it'll run. Get in." As he opened the door for me, it fell down slightly on one hinge, but he pulled it up, saying, "You have to know how. These are tricky doors." When he got the car in motion, he sat back rather happily. This was long before seat belts, but I sure could have used one! "You know," he said, "some months ago I couldn't have afforded even a car like this. I haven't moved far up the scale, but I'll tell you one thing: this car is paid for."

Then, in a quieter tone, he said, "I want to tell you a story of spiritual victory. I was a failure. I was frustrated. Everything I did ultimately went wrong. I'd start out all right. Then I'd do some stupid thing. I'd get into a wrangle with someone. Or I would say something out of line, or I'd get into some dishonesty. I made a mess of one thing after another. My wife finally got disgusted and left me. Then I took to drink, and what little money I had left disappeared. I was down, completely down.

"At this point, a friend came to me and said, 'Frank, you don't need to be this way. You have abilities and you can live a successful life, if you'll do one thing.' And he led me to Jesus Christ. I accepted Christ; I took Him into my life; I committed my whole self to Him. My friend said to me, 'Frank, I want you to read the Bible. But I don't want you to read the whole Bible yet, because you'd get mixed up; you'd get lost. I want you to stick to Matthew, Mark, Luke, and John, and read every word of those four books. And when you come to a passage that particularly strikes you, I want you to commit that passage to memory.'

"So I started reading. One day, I came upon a passage where Jesus is saying to Peter, 'I will give unto thee the keys of the kingdom of heaven' [Matthew 16:19]. That fascinated me, because I knew Peter also had messed up his life and even denied the Lord, just as I had. But the Lord said to Peter, 'I will give unto thee the keys of the kingdom of heaven.' I took it as meaning He would give the keys to me, too, and I began to ask myself what He meant by the kingdom of heaven. I reasoned that the kingdom of heaven must be full of God's love, full of His peace, full of His rightness, full of every good thing. Each day in my prayers, I unlocked the kingdom of heaven, and these marvelous blessings started flowing into my life. This hasn't brought me much money, but it wasn't designed to bring me money."

> *One way prayer can change your life is by*
> *teaching you to think creatively. . . .*
> *Prayer sharpens the mind. . . .*

When we rattled up to the door of my hotel and he let me out, he said, "Hang on to those keys." And, when we had said good-night, he slammed the car door (which nearly fell off in the process). I watched him move out into the traffic.

In my mind, that battered old car was invested with the splendor of a chariot being driven by a knight in shining armor. That man had had his life changed. He found Jesus Christ and accepted Him as his Savior, and then he learned to pray in such a way that he developed perception and understanding.

One way prayer can change your life is by teaching you to think creatively. The way you think spells the difference between living well and living poorly. Prayer sharpens the mind and thereby brings the believer into harmony with the great Mind.

Prayer is a mental process. If you have the idea that it is merely the mumbling of a few words, I almost think you're better off not to use it at all, for that degrades it. True prayer requires discipline, pain, and agony of thought. But when you do think prayerfully, with Jesus as your guide, you break free from defeats.

I believe any problem, any defeat, and any difficulty can be overcome through prayer. I have a friend who runs a big bakery business that he built from small beginnings. He was the company's first baker. As a matter of fact, he claims he can still make better bread and cakes than most of the present bakers. One day, he described to me a significant experience he had some years ago. He had been faced with an extremely worrisome problem. He would pace the floor trying to figure out a solution. He lay awake nights brooding over it. Then one day, as he sat in his office feeling completely baffled, he chanced to glance at his mother's picture on the wall.

"My mother," he told me, "was a Kansas woman reared on the farm where I was born. She was tall and gaunt. She never was able to beautify herself much. She was just a plain woman all her life. But she was wise. She never had much schooling. But in the hard, good life she and my father lived together, she learned many things in the school of experience. And she used to say to us children, 'When you have a problem, and you've worked as hard as you can at it, given it all you've got, and still you haven't solved it, the thing to do is just walk away from it and think about God. But don't talk to God about the problem. Talk to Him about Himself. Tell Him how much you love Him. Talk to Jesus and thank Him for all He has done for you. Tell Him you want to be His faithful follower. Have fellowship with God and with Jesus.' "

How wise that woman was—maybe wiser than she knew! For when you concentrate on a problem unduly long and do not get the answer, you tense up, your thinking freezes, and neither insights nor ideas come through. You must then let it be for a while, to break the strain. After that, when you talk to Jesus about it, you will find that He lifts you way up so when you go back to the problem, you have grown and the problem shrinks. Then, prayerfully, you can break it open and find the right answer.

So my friend, in his perplexity, looked at the picture of his mother, departed long since but still living and still speaking to him in thought. And he decided to leave the problem for a while. He took out his Bible and read passages his mother had marked in it. He thought about Jesus and he rededicated himself, acknowledging that he felt he had not been growing spiritually as he ought, that he'd been less than himself. After a time, he turned back to the problem. Did he get an answer immediately? No. But now he felt calm about it. He was confident he would somehow be able to handle it. And later he did find a satisfactory solution.

Often a person will complain, "I've prayed and prayed and I didn't get what I wanted." Well, who said you are supposed to get what you want? Prayer isn't a device to get what you want. Prayer is a means of bringing you to the point where you will accept what God wants. If you're using prayer just for getting what you want, you're engaging in an improper use of it. The Lord does want good things for us and, if with all your heart you pray for something that is wholesome and constructive, you are likely to receive it. Sometimes the thing you pray for is something you shouldn't have. We are like children; we want what we want, when we want it. This infantilism is in most of us. To be a Christian means to be a mature person. You learn to say, "This is what I'd like to have, Lord, if You think it's all right for me; but if You don't, then give me what You want me to have, or show me what You want me to do."

I met a lady who said to me, "I have been to your church twice and heard two of your sermons." She sounded so enthusiastic that I thought she was going to tell me those sermons had done her a lot of good. But she didn't. "I also heard your wife make a speech," she said, "at the church I belong to—and that is what I really remember."

"Well, that is not surprising to me," I said. "I get most of my good ideas from my wife." That's teamwork, you know. If you have a wife you pray with, and work with, and walk the pathway of life with, and she and you try to serve the Lord together, you don't know where one begins and the other leaves off.

At any rate, this woman explained that she had been struggling in prayer for something she wanted, and God wasn't answering her prayers. And Mrs. Peale, in that speech, had remarked that there are three ways God answers prayer: Yes. Wait awhile. No. "And when she said that," the woman told me, "I knew I had my answer. It was no. But I hadn't wanted to take a *no* answer."

"Maybe that *no* answer is going to lead you to some great experience," I said. "And when you love Him enough to trust Him, you humbly say, 'All right, Lord, I accept that, and I look to You for further guidance.' Then some bright day you realize, 'If He had not said no, this wonderful thing I now have would not have come to me.' "

The attitude that really leads to life in all its fullness is that of a child walking with Him, loving Him, trusting Him, seeking to serve Him. Prayer, in this attitude, can change your life wonderfully.

THIRTEEN
COME ALIVE!

People have different ideas of the Christian faith. For one thing, it is the way of eternal salvation. I often think of it also as a sort of hospital where any person, wounded in body, mind, or soul, may come for healing and renewal. It is a source of energy, enabling any who are tired, discouraged, or frustrated to receive an injection of power. It is an enthusiasm builder. When you have a down attitude toward yourself or toward life, Christian faith will rejuvenate you.

So many of us suffer from tired, gloomy, desultory thoughts, with the result that our life force is reduced. Of course, we have been infused by the media over a long time with such thoughts. Years ago, there was a popular radio commentator in my neighborhood. He had a great voice. But every time he started a radio program, he would say, "There's bad news tonight, folks." He claimed to be an objective reporter and was merely telling it as it was. It became his trademark: "There's bad news tonight."

His successors have surpassed him. They not only come up with bad news but also are pushing pessimistic and cynical viewpoints. With people telling us "there is bad news" all the time, it is a wonder that the country survives. Here's some bad news I cut from a magazine called *Success:*

It is a gloomy moment in the history of our country. Not in the lifetime of most men has there been so much grave and deep apprehension; never has the future seemed so incalculable as at this time. The domestic economic situation is in chaos. Our dollar is weak throughout the world. Prices are so high as to be utterly impossible. The political cauldron seethes and bubbles with uncertainty. It is a solemn moment of our troubles. No man can see the end.

I suppose some might agree that this is a fairly accurate picture of today. However, that was first published in *Harper's Weekly* in October 1857. It's a wonder the country has survived all this bad news!

Our ancestors, I believe, were tougher than we are. They had substantial faith and were able to separate the temporary from the eternal. As thinkers, they knew that humanity goes forward by difficulty, pain, and suffering. But they also knew that if you stick it out, if you keep your faith in God, if you do your part as a citizen and as a Christian, no matter how many dark clouds may appear, the sun will shine again. So, let us be rid of those tired and gloomy thoughts and come alive. Get the pollution of negative thinking out of your mind. The world is good. People are good. The future is good. Of course, that is not to say there is no bad news along with it. But humanity has gone forward by overcoming bad news.

Such victories represent much of the history of Christianity. It was born in a bad-news time. Indeed, it has grown great in bad-news eras. It becomes greater whenever it has to deal with bad-news situations. For faith draws upon a power that is of the essence of time. We are in the timeless, not the ephemeral, time equation.

Most of us have been affected by these tired, gloomy thoughts, and all of us would like to be rid of them and come alive. How do you do it? First, an important and effective technique is to constantly practice being *under-whelmed*, not overwhelmed. Everyone, in effect, exclaims, "This overwhelms me. That situation overwhelms me; our country is overwhelmed with problems, taxes, and a huge deficit."

Now, what do you get by being overwhelmed? All you do is create additional tension. The idea is to be under-whelmed. The secret is to *de-emotionalize* yourself. One great trouble with contemporary life is that we have so many superemotionalized people. The antidote to that is to think rather than to be emotional. Any problem can be solved if a person will keep cool and think. That is all you have to do. Just think and pray, for prayer is a form of thought; prayers bring divine intelligence to aid your own intelligence. The human mind will not function effectively when it is super-heated by emotion; only when the mind is cool, rational, dispassionate, and underwhelmed will it produce logical concepts. The human mind *can* get answers to difficulties. So don't get into a tizzy. Don't be in a dither. Don't emotionalize. Think!

I was once in a hotel where I was to speak at a luncheon. They told me 910 people were signed up for this luncheon.

I was sitting in the office of the manager, an old friend of mine, when his assistant came rushing in. He was perspiring and red of face. "We are in a bad situation," he said.

The manager calmly said, "Jim, tell me about it."

"We have one thousand twenty people and are prepared for nine hundred ten. What will we do?"

"I'll tell you what to do, Jim," said the manager. "The tables in the ballroom are now too far apart. Put them closer together by six inches and that will give you the space you need. If necessary, put some tables in the foyer outside the dining room."

"Well," the assistant agreed, "maybe we can do that, but what about the food? We don't have enough for a thousand twenty people. We are serving roast beef and it won't go around."

The manager replied, "Set the gauge on the cutting machine and slice the beef a little thinner."

"But we're serving peas."

"Well," the manager asked, "how many peas are you giving a person?"

"We count out one hundred peas to every person." (I thought that was a lot of peas, but that is what he said.)

"Make it ninety," the manager said, "and you're in."

"But," the man still objected, "we don't have enough rolls. We have to put a roll on every plate."

"Oh, no, you don't; pass the rolls. Half the diners won't take a roll."

The assistant manager calmed down, wiped the perspiration from his brow, and went out. The manager sat back, put his feet up on the desk, and said, "You know something? One of the secrets of this hotel business is to know how to be calm in a crisis. Never let anything work you up. There is always an answer to everything if you will just keep calm and think," and then he added, "and pray." Then he said, with a serious look on his face, "I pray about my job every day."

I went into the luncheon and the meat was delicious. (I would have been glad to settle for forty of the peas they had.) Underwhelmed! That's the idea.

Now, the world isn't going to go to pieces; nor is the United States; nor is your business; nor is your life. It never has and it never will—if you get rid of all those old, tired, gloomy thoughts. Isaiah was so right: "In confidence and quietness shall be your strength" (*see* Isaiah 30:15).

In San Francisco, I was a guest on a call-in radio talk show. I don't like talk shows because you never know what kind of question you're going to get and you never know what kind of answer you're going to give. On this show, a man called and asked, "Dr. Peale, is that you?"

"Yes, sir, that's right."

"You're sure it's you?"

"As far as I know it's me."

"You always talk about positive thinking, don't you?"

"Not always. I refer to it occasionally."

"Well," he continued, "I don't buy that positive thinking! I have a problem you can't get around. You might as well fold up on this because you can't handle it."

I replied, "If that is the case, why go further with it?"

"I want to get an answer. Here is the question: I'm fifty-two years of age and out of a job. You know yourself that no man fifty-two years old can get a job. Furthermore, I don't have any brains. I haven't had any good experience. I haven't had any education and no one likes me. What are you going to tell me to do about that?"

I asked, "How do you know you haven't any brains?"

"When I was young, I was told I didn't have any brains. The brains in the family all went to my brother."

"Who told you that?"

"My brother."

"But you sound to me as if you have brains."

Then I continued, "Are you telling me that no one fifty-two can get a job? I hired a man just last week who was fifty-nine years old. The trouble is, you're overwhelmed. If you get underwhelmed, I know you can get a job." I took another angle: "Who did you say doesn't like you?"

"No one likes me."

"Do you like yourself?"

"I never thought about that."

"If you will get to like yourself as a child of God, you will realize that you have what it takes to get a job and do a great job." Then I added, "You must love your neighbor as yourself. But you can't love your neighbor until you love yourself."

Finally, he asked, "Will you pray for me?"

"Now you're talking! Of course I'll pray for you, and you pray for yourself."

Then he asked, "Is that positive thinking?"

"No, that's just faith in yourself and faith in a good God, but it certainly isn't *negative* thinking."

About six weeks later, I had a note from this man saying he had a job. He said, "It isn't much of a job, but believe me, by the time I get through with it, I'll make a terrific job out of it!"

That's the way to think and talk! Take what you can get, and do the best you can with it. Work at it until it becomes something great. There are negative-talking, miserable, defeated, unhappy, discouraged people everywhere. It isn't necessary to be that way, either about yourself or about your country or about the time in which you live. So say to yourself and to your husband or wife, "You know something, honey, from now on I am underwhelmed." Of course, you may shake him up for a while, but he'll get used to it. *Underwhelmed* is the word.

Once you become underwhelmed, get excited about life. Are you excited? Could you honestly tell yourself that when you arose on this beautiful morning, you were excited? You weren't? That is indeed a pity! But you may ask, "What do you mean? I can't turn on excitement at will. If you're excited, you're excited. If you're not excited, you're not excited. You can't go to the drugstore and buy a bottle of excitement."

Well, listen. If you are not excited, you can get excited. How? Act as if you are excited. This is one of the greatest psychological principles ever enunciated. It was first mentioned in this country by nineteenth-century philosopher William James, who at one time was a Harvard professor of anatomy, psychology, and philosophy (body, mind, and soul, you might say). He taught the "As If" principle. That is to say, if you're full of fear and you want to be full of courage instead, you must act "as if" you did have courage and, in due course, you will be courageous.

And if you're full of hate and want to change—you want to love people, instead—act "as if" you are loving, and presently, in the very nature of the psychology of the human being, you will begin to take on loving aspects. So if you're not excited, act as if you are excited. Go out and say, "Isn't this a terrific day? Look at that sky! Look at those beautiful clouds! Feel that wonderful rain on my face!" Do this and you will become excited.

This is what our faith is designed to do: lift us up into excitement about life. What is a preacher's job? It is to build people up in faith so they will be excited about God, about Jesus Christ, about themselves, about other people, about their world, about their day and their generation. Get excited! You're never going to live this day again. Never again! So live it to the hilt.

That reminds me of a professor at Syracuse University, Dean Hugh Tilroe of the College of Public Speaking, an outstanding orator in upstate New York. He was one of the men who installed me as pastor of a church in Syracuse. I didn't know who he was, that first Sunday; while sitting with him in the pulpit, I leaned over and asked, "Professor, what do you teach in the university?"

He said, "Public speaking."

"Oh, my," I groaned.

"Don't let me bother you," he said. "I've made speeches for so long I know how nerve-racking it is. I'm not here judging you. I'm your friend. Tell the people out in front what you know about Jesus Christ and tell them to be enthusiastic and excited."

So I tried to do the best I could. And I loved this man from that moment on.

> *The world belongs to the enthusiasts*
>
> *who can keep cool.*

A few years later, I received a telephone call and was told that he had suffered a stroke. When I visited him, he was lying in bed and not even able to raise his hand. His speech was slurred. He was like a great big oak tree that had fallen.

"I—I can't hunt anymore." (He was a great hunter.) "I can't fish anymore." (He was also a great fisherman.) "I can't teach anymore; can't speak anymore." And he added, "I have a date tomorrow night in Pennsylvania for a commencement. I want you to go and substitute for me."

"What do you want me to tell them, Professor?"

"Tell them to love the Lord and be enthusiastic and excited. Tell them that excitement sweeps every resistance before it. Tell them to love the world, to love people; tell them to be excited."

I could hardly bear seeing him lying there, broken like

that. I went out and walked up and down Walnut Avenue, weeping because this great man, my friend, had fallen. And I went to Pennsylvania the next night and talked about excitement and enthusiasm in memory of him.

The two suggestions I have mentioned—underwhelmed and excitement—are important, for the world belongs to the enthusiasts who can keep cool. Never become gloomy; never lose faith. Always believe in the possibilities inherent in human nature. Always believe in the greatness of yourself. Forever believe in the future of mankind. Be a believer, an enthusiast, an excited person who doesn't emotionalize but always keeps cool. Trust the Lord and think!

Whenever I recall my old friend Hugh Tilroe, broken physically but not mentally or spiritually, his advice comes back to me: "In God's name, tell people that they are great souls, that they can be greater people, that life is good, and that it can be greater by overcoming bad news."

Visualize now those tired, gloomy thoughts flowing out of your mind, leaving you underwhelmed by all the bad news. Think objectively and dispassionately. Do not emotionalize but *think*. Be excited and life will be good, very good.

FOURTEEN

"I'LL SEE YOU IN THE MORNING"

It was a long-distance telephone call, spanning nearly half the continent. The voice at one end was feminine, old, and frail. The voice at the other end was masculine, vital, and crisply strong. It was an aged mother and a beyond-middle-aged son who were speaking.

Strangely and tenderly, sometimes I grant you exasperatingly, men to mothers are always little boys. The conversation, therefore, was pitched on that level, and she talked to him about the simple, humble, endearing things of the family. She was talking from a little midwestern village, from an old-fashioned home on a tree-lined street. He was in a towering office building in throbbing and surging Manhattan. But it was a communication between two people who loved each other more than life itself.

He knew she wasn't well and he said to her, "Mother, I am flying out tonight and we will have a good time together. You just get everything ready and I will be with you tomorrow."

"Ah," she said, "I will have all the things you like to eat.

Won't it be nice to have my boy home again?" And then her quavering voice came over the phone, "I'll see you in the morning."

When he arrived the next morning, he was told that, quietly and peacefully during the night, his beloved mother had gone across to the other side. There she lay peacefully. He looked upon her face, upon the lips that would not speak again, and he knew that the last words he had heard her say he would never forget: "I'll see you in the morning."

This man is a longtime friend of mine—modern, businesslike, matter-of-fact; you might even say he is sophisticated. I once asked him what he thought about that phrase, "I'll see you in the morning." He looked at me with a face full of surprise. "Why, of course," he said, "I'll see her in the morning."

"How do you know?" I asked.

"Oh," he replied, "don't you remember how you and I and our other friends used to go to those little country churches long ago?" And I do well remember. I thank the Lord that I had a chance to grow up in little country churches just after the turn of the century. Looking out the windows, you saw no buildings, only fields and hills and woods and the sky.

Those preachers weren't always highly educated men, but they believed everything they said. Furthermore, they had spiritual experience to communicate; they were talking from lives that knew God through Jesus Christ. My friend continued, "Don't you remember the dear old hymn, 'There's a land that is fairer than day, And by faith we can see it

afar.' And the refrain: 'In the sweet by and by, We shall
meet on that beautiful shore.' Oh, yes," he said, "I haven't
the slightest doubt at all that I will see her in the morning."

When I first began preaching, we had to deal with crass,
sophomoric, cocky scientists who had suddenly discovered
the amazing things man could do in the universe. They
tended to bow God out, or at least reduce Him. They
treated the Bible (at least some did) as old wives' tales.
People who had a fundamental concept of God were looked
upon askance. Thus began a slow but steady abandonment
of the precepts of the faith. Science, you see, had to grow
up, and it took quite a few years.

I used to think that, in an Easter sermon, I had to spend
half my time defending the faith. I got over that a long
while ago, and so did science, because science now has
reached out in this universe and found that it is a revelation
of God rather than a depreciation of Him. It is increasingly
apparent that the whole universe is, and can be, characterized by one word, *life,* and not the word *death.* So the

> No one has to prove the Bible. The Bible
> has long since proved itself.

ancient Gospel comes back now with the support of science.

If you are so old-fashioned and outmoded as to want to
raise a conflict between science and religion, you ought to

go back to school. Science now shows that in this universe is a vast Mind and a great Spirit. The great men have always held this view; it was only the small-fry, scientific infantile who said that science and Christianity were incompatible.

I once went on archeological expeditions in the Holy Land with some of the greatest scholars in this field. I asked one of them, "Are you trying to prove the Bible?"

"We are pure scientists," he replied. "We are working to uncover what is here. We are not digging to prove anything." Then he looked at me and asked, "What is the matter with you? No one has to prove the Bible. The Bible has long since proved itself. But I will tell you one thing for sure: Everything we uncover substantiates what the Bible says about the circumstances of the ancient life with which we are working."

So, if the Bible tells you that there is a land beyond, that there is life after death, that there is immortality, you can be sure it is a fact. And the great minds have always known it. Take John Morely who, at the end of his remarkable book of recollections, writes: "And so to my home and in the gathering twilight." What home? Why, of course, the many mansions beyond this life of mortality.

Years ago, Sir William Osler gave a speech to the students at Yale that has gone down in history as a classic. He has been characterized as the greatest doctor who ever practiced in the United States. Born in Canada, later he taught at Johns Hopkins University and finally in England. When he decided to leave the United States, the greatest financiers in the country offered large sums to keep him here. He trained the famous Mayo brothers and Harvey Cushing, the great brain surgeon.

Dr. Osler lost a son in World War I. The greatest physicians in the American army tried to save the boy, but his wounds were mortal. Sadly, they had to put in the earth the body of the beloved son of their dear chief. This was the beginning of the end for Osler, for the boy was the apple of his eye, the idol of his life, the center of his dreams. Finally, a few years later, Osler was taken with an illness which he, with his skillful understanding and marvelous diagnostic ability, knew to be a fatal disease. He was observed, in his last hours, writing something on a sheet of paper. When he was dead, they had to take the paper from his cold hands, and this is what it said: "And so the voyage is nearly over and the harbor in view. It has been a glorious journey with such good companions along the way. But, I go gladly, for my boy will be waiting for me over there."

Now, are you willing to presume that a mind like Sir William Osler's was wrong, especially when his faith was

> *There has never been any darkness*
> *that hasn't given way to light.*

built upon the substantiality of the Word of God and the permanency of Jesus of Nazareth, as well as human intellectual and spiritual history? No one anywhere has yet disproved Jesus. He lives, and because He lives, we live also.

So, when you have to come to that sad experience of seeing someone whom you love disappear into the darkness, just listen and you will hear that person say, "I'll see you in the morning." And when the time comes that you, too, shall go into that darkness, realize to your comfort that darkness is only the prelude to light.

Did you ever observe that there has never been any darkness that hasn't given way to light? Light is the ruler of the day, the sun; light is the answer, not darkness. I was at Mount Holyoke College once, visiting my daughter Elizabeth, who was a student there. We were walking around the campus of this lovely New England college and came upon a sundial which had the following inscription: "To larger sight the rim of shadow is the line of light." We meditated on it and discussed it. There was no author's name given and no explanation offered.

With small sight, you see only shadow; to larger sight, the rim of shadow is the line or beginning of light. That is exactly what the Resurrection story teaches.

Let me illustrate this further. I went out to Kennedy Airport one night to take a plane to Paris. We took off quite late due to some mechanical difficulty; in fact, it was one o'clock in the morning. It was a moonless and starless night. There was rain in the air and some mist; it was very black and dark. That is really something, isn't it, to get into a mighty plane and zoom through the dark, heading east over the dark ocean. The attendant came around to pull down the window shades, and I said to her, "Please leave mine up; I want to see what I can see."

I sat there looking into the darkness and faintly, far in the distance—you see it was then 6:00 A.M. in Paris—a thin line of golden light appeared. Five hundred miles and one hour later, all of a sudden that line of light burst into the amazing glory of the dawn.

That is the way it is. When the final hour comes, and the deep darkness is there, remember the words on the sundial: "To larger sight the rim of shadow is the line of light." "I'll see you in the morning."

Many have had mystical experiences along this line. I was preaching in Georgia at a Methodist gathering under the leadership of my good friend Bishop Arthur Moore. He had some Methodist preachers of Georgia there with their church members. It was a real old-time Methodist gathering, and such preaching! Dr. Charles Allen of Houston, Texas, a lanky, dyed-in-the-wool Southerner, was just wonderful, and so was Bishop Moore, one of the truly great preachers of our time. And I came along with my poor little feeble Yankee talk. And there was lots of singing.

At the end of the final meeting, Bishop Moore asked all the preachers in the congregation to come to the platform and form a choir to sing for the folks. As they came, the congregation was singing that old song, "At the cross, at the cross where I first saw the light, And the burden of my heart rolled away." As these preachers walked down from their places, I was sitting on the platform. They all walked down the aisles, singing that old hymn. Then I saw my dear old father.

Before he died, my father had suffered several strokes and could hardly move, and his voice was a whisper. But as I was sitting on that platform, there walked my father down the aisle, singing, with a wonderful light on his face: "At the cross, at the cross where I first saw the light." He seemed about forty; he was trim and vital and healthy and handsome, and he was smiling at me. When he put up his hand in the old familiar gesture, it was so real that I jumped up from my chair. What other people thought, I don't know. But there were only my father and I in that big auditorium. Then I sat down and could see him no more; but the inner feeling of his presence in my heart was indisputable. So I can say to my dear father, "I'll see you in the morning."

There is just one more thing about this great Resurrection truth that I wish to emphasize. Why was Jesus Christ raised from the dead? To prove that nothing can overcome the power of God—nothing—not even death.

What I should like to ask you, and ask myself, is this: Are you, and am I, living in the power of this Resurrection? Or are we defeated? My simple belief about Christianity is that if you really get it in your heart, it gives you an astonishing power. The trouble is that most of us have only a weak version of it. But get the resurrected kind of faith, and you really have something that can defeat anything.

Let me illustrate that possession of power by those who live in the power of the Resurrection. I once sat in my study with a tiny woman. She sat on my couch and her feet didn't even touch the floor. She was dressed in a Chinese costume, but she was British. She had that wonderful cockney speech that I always liked. One day, in London, she went to a Salvation Army street meeting and was converted; and when I say converted, I mean converted. She became a resurrected person. Then she developed an avid interest. The gentleman for whom she worked had a wonderful library on China and she began reading.

One day, her employer came in and found her reading and reproached her. He said, "I hired you to dust and clean, not to read my books. Besides, you didn't ask if you might read my books."

"Ah, sir," she said, "I am so fascinated with China."

"Read the books, but not until after you get the housework done," he replied.

Then she received the call. She believed that God wanted her to go as a missionary to China. She went to the Mission Board and, of course, they were all highly intellectual, highly educated ecclesiastics, and they gave her an intellectual test that she couldn't pass. They said no, you do not measure up to our intellectual standards; you can't go. But did that faze her? Not at all. She had received her commission from a higher Source than a Mission Board.

So remarkable was the career of the missionary Gladys Aylward that, years later, a motion picture was made of it called *Inn of the Sixth Happiness.* And it was a fascinating movie. This Gladys Aylward, sitting in my study, told me about the times she used to preach on the streets in

Yencheng and other Chinese cities. The little British cockney woman told the people that no power on earth could
overcome the Christian, that God was with him and Jesus
Christ was with him and that, if he would become a resurrected soul, he could triumph over the world. This went on,
week after week.

One day, the governor summoned her and said, "We
have a terrible situation. There is a riot in the prison, where
murderers and vicious men are guarded by only twelve sol-
diers. We can't go in; they will kill us. And one of the worst
men in the prison is berserk. He has a huge meat cleaver in
his hand and has already killed two men and terrified the
others. We want you to go in and take the meat cleaver out
of his hands."

"You must be out of your mind, sir," she said.

"I have listened to you in the street telling that your God
is always with you, about Daniel in the lion's den, and how
Jesus Christ, in your heart, will protect you."

"Ah, but you misunderstand, sir."

"Oh, you haven't been telling the truth," he replied. "I
only know what I heard you say and I believed you."

She knew then that, if she ever wanted to preach again,
she would have to go into that prison. She asked the Lord to
go with her and she felt strangely peaceful. She stood at the
prison door; they unlocked it, quickly shut it, so fearful
were they. She found herself in a long, narrow tunnel. At
the end, she could see men wildly running about, shouting
and cursing. She prayed, "Be within me, Jesus."

She walked to the end of the tunnel and saw the madman,

the meat cleaver dripping with blood, chasing a man. Suddenly he was in front of her. They stood facing each other, the little woman and the giant. She looked into his wild and feverish eyes and calmly said, "Give me that weapon." There was a moment of hesitation; then, with utter docility, he handed it to her. "Now," she said, "get in line, all of you men—get back in line." Quietly, they lined up.

Addressing them, she asked, "What are your complaints? I will tell them to the governor and I assure you in his name that, where possible, they will be corrected."

The resurrected life, the Resurrection of Jesus Christ, is to give us spiritual power for ourselves and all the world, and the power to make a better world in His name. All who live with Him can be sure of meeting again those you love and have lost awhile. You may confidently say to them, "I'll see you in the morning."

FIFTEEN
MIRACULOUS LOVE

A group of us stood on a hillside overlooking some fields where occurred one of the greatest events in the history of mankind. In those fields, on a mystic and starlit night long ago, some simple shepherds saw the heavens filled with a chorus of angels proclaiming peace on earth, goodwill to men.

I contemplated those fields, remembering that the shepherds, after viewing that angelic sight, said, "Let us now go even unto Bethlehem, and see this thing which is come to pass" (Luke 2:15). And then our group, too, went to Bethlehem, a short distance away.

In that land, changes take place slowly. Camel trains are still silhouetted against the sky; people still ride little donkeys; shepherds still watch over their flocks by day and night, on rocky hillsides and in stony pastures.

There is, in the Holy Land, a strange blending of the old with the new. I saw a train of fifty camels, laden with merchandise and led by an Arab in flowing white garments with a voluminous headdress shielding his face from the sun. The camel train pulled up and stopped for a red light at the Jerusalem airport to let an airplane taxi in from a faraway place. The Arab was unmoved by the airplane.

> *The miracle is not only His birth*
> *but also what He does.*

When the light changed to green, the camels moved on.

At another place, I saw a sweet-faced young mother riding a donkey and holding a baby in her arms. The donkey was led by a sturdy young man clad in traditional costume. The couple seemed to me for all the world like Mary and Joseph coming into that ancient walled town.

At Bethlehem, our group lingered silently and thoughtfully at the place where Jesus was born. The land is honeycombed with the caves in which people then lived. Jesus probably wasn't born in a wooden stable as we know stables here but in a cave where the animals were sheltered.

It is the same little town of Bethlehem over which the star stood, where the everlasting light proclaimed that here had taken place the greatest miracle of all. And the miracle is not only His birth but also what He does. From time to time, people tell me that miracles never happen. I used to agree with them because I wanted to be scientific. But I finally decided that the highest form of science is spiritual science, for it follows laws the same as physical science does; and Jesus Christ releases powers in history greater than any that physical science has ever released.

A miracle is a wonder that we find difficult to explain. After we have learned to explain it, we no longer regard it as a miracle. One of these miracles is the miracle of love. Haven't you ever noticed the strange things that seem to happen to people at Christmastime? On Christmas Eve, for example, amid the throngs on the city streets, irritation is softened and stridencies become less. There is a flow of love, a community of understanding. Prejudice weakens and, for twenty-four hours, cities, towns, and villages everywhere are different because people's hearts are different. I have never known this to fail. In all my years, I have often wondered why all of us could not be this way throughout the year. It is the miracle of love working magical transformations.

When I began preaching, businesspeople and scientists— indeed almost everyone—thought of love as something theoretical. Now, however, scientists and the so-called realistic thinkers tell us that the only practical way to live is by practicing love and goodwill.

Yet I have always known that love really works. On one of our early trips to Jerusalem, the Holy City, we saw people fighting one another. In the center of the city there was an eight-hundred-foot stretch of desolation called No Man's Land. On one side were warring Arabs, on the other, warring Jews.

I was waiting at this No Man's Land checkpoint to meet Father Patrick, a famous Franciscan priest. Finally, an old car chugging along was stopped by the sentry. Out of the car stepped a priest with a face that made you love him at once. Father Patrick was one of the best-known Christians in the Middle East. He could even cross the border unchallenged. At this meeting, the sentries gathered around him and he put his arm around them, saying, "Hi, boys! How are you all?"

I said to one of the sentries, "You fellows seem to love Father Patrick."

"Oh, yes, we all love him," he replied.

One of them waved an arm toward the other side. "They love him over there," he said, "just as we do here."

This Franciscan was going back and forth, weaving strands of love that no politician could weave, that no United Nations commissioners could bring about! It was a living demonstration that on those very roadways where Jesus walked, there was occurring a miracle of love. A modern disciple, Father Patrick demonstrated that people can learn to live together in goodwill.

Perhaps the idea of love working internationally in the relationships between peoples may surprise you. It should not. Have you ever actually, wholeheartedly, tried love instead of hate? When someone has done something that has annoyed or offended you, have you ever tried loving him into a good relationship instead of fighting him back? Did you ever bless people for the mean things they have done to you? Have you ever overcome your prejudices and preconceived notions about people by learning to know and love them?

A man spoke to me once in a city where I was scheduled to speak. I recognized him as the assistant to a seemingly very difficult executive in a midwestern business. This assistant, Bill, I will call him, had to report to his boss every day. "I would actually stand outside his door feeling cold all over," Bill told me. "My hands were clammy. I could feel chills going up and down my spine. And I knew he would either bark at me or receive me in stony silence.

" 'There, sir, there it is,' I would say, placing my report before him.

"He would look at it, then at me, and never say a word. Sometimes he would grumble, 'All right. Get going. I have it.' "

Of course this attitude stimulated a feeling of hatred within the assistant. He asked me what he ought to do. "Perhaps, if we were of the same faith, we might get together," he said.

"Well," I replied, "you are of the same faith in God. That makes you his brother. Have you brought the Bible to bear on the situation? I suggest that you try loving that man into a pleasant relationship."

"No one can love him," he protested. "There isn't a soul in the world who loves him."

"Then perhaps he is suffering from an inferiority complex," I suggested. "Maybe he is lonely and shy, and his spirit has retreated behind this domineering personality. Why don't you try an experiment? Pray for him, asking that you may understand him and be able to help him. Put tomorrow's meeting with him in God's hands. Think of this unhappy man and forget yourself, and when you stand outside his door in the morning, project thoughts of love toward him. Ask the Lord how you can help him."

Bill tried the experiment for a long time without results. Then, while they were discussing a problem in cost accounting, a subject in which Bill was an expert, they were bending over the desks, their heads close together. "Suddenly I felt a surge of love like a wave of compassion sweeping over me," Bill told me later. "And when we had finished our discussion, the boss put his hand on my shoulder and said, 'Bill, I've come to depend upon you more and more. You mean a lot to me.' In that moment I saw, behind the stern exterior, the unhappy, lonely man you had suggested he might be."

Bill is no longer shrinking and inarticulate. "I want to tell you," he declared, "this power of love works. People I once disliked or looked down upon, I now appreciate and get along with."

That is what the Baby, born in a manger long ago, came to tell us. I have often wondered about the wondrous power given Him at birth, which He exercised over human beings. Some mysterious quality was put into Jesus—into His smile, into His voice—so that people, when they came close to Him, were changed completely. As they yielded themselves to Jesus, no matter what their weaknesses and failures had been, they were taken away. This is the greatest miracle of all—this new birth that takes place within human beings.

I don't know what your life struggle may have been, what weakness, what sense of defeat, or what prejudice has plagued you. You know what they are. You may have struggled with them all your life and been defeated by them. But the minute you yield yourself to the Spirit of Him who first came as a Baby in a manger, you can be changed.

> *Most unhappy people simply need the love and understanding of others who have the spiritual answer.*

A wonderful story showing the application of brotherhood and love is revealed by an incident that occurred in a hospital when a hopeless, battered, would-be suicide was brought in. A nurse, in talking to him, discovered that he knew a great deal about medicine. She spoke to the attending physician. "I think this poor fellow is a doctor," she said.

"Where did you get your medical information?" the doctor asked the patient.

"Never mind," was the answer. But the doctor pursued the subject. "You interest me. You have learned a lot somewhere." Eventually, the man opened up and told his story.

"I was a lieutenant colonel in the medical department of the army," the man admitted. "I practiced medicine in a large city before the war."

"What happened to you?" the physician asked.

"My wife was unfaithful to me, and it knocked the props out from under me. From then on, I didn't care and I just let myself go. I became an alcoholic. Now I'm licked, hopeless. I wish you would let me die."

The physician remembered that Freddie, an orderly, had been brought into the hospital in the same hopeless condition. But Freddie had found Christ. So the doctor sent for Freddie to talk to the man.

Freddie told the patient, "You can never do anything for yourself. But if you will just let Jesus heal you, He can put you right back where you were; maybe He'll do even better by you."

The patient stared intently at Freddie's face. "I heard that as a boy," he said, "but I never gave myself to Jesus."

"You will never know peace until you do," the orderly insisted.

"How do you do it?" asked the man.

Freddie told him. "All you need to say is, 'Dear Jesus, I am weak and can't handle my life. I give myself to You.' "

Sometime later, that patient was successfully practicing his profession again. That is why, all over the world, people are singing about Jesus. That is the reason we love Him so. What is His power? It is the power of God, who created us and is always re-creating us. Most unhappy people simply need the love and understanding of others who have the spiritual answer.

If you are doing what you know is wrong or mean or unkind, if you feel weakness or inability within yourself, just give yourself to Him. These things will fall away and you will be made new in Christ. That is why the shepherds said, "Let us now go even unto Bethlehem, and see this thing which is come to pass."

Miracles do happen, even today.

ABOUT THE AUTHOR

Dr. Norman Vincent Peale, author of the bestseller *The Power of Positive Thinking* and over 45 other books, was once called "the most widely read inspirational author of a generation." He was the pastor of Marble Collegiate Church in New York City and founder of Guideposts Associates, *Guideposts* magazine, and the Peale Center for Christian Living. He passed away in 1993.